William Ezelle Jones

Monumental Silver: Selections from the Gilbert Collection

Los Angeles County Museum of Art   28 April–10 July 1977

Published by the
Los Angeles County Museum of Art
5905 Wilshire Boulevard
Los Angeles, California 90036

Copyright © 1977 by
Museum Associates of the
Los Angeles County Museum of Art

Library of Congress Cataloging in Publication Data

Los Angeles Co., Calif.
Museum of Art, Los Angeles.
Monumental silver.

Bibliography: p.
1.
Silverwork—Exhibitions.
2.
Gilbert, Arthur, 1913–   —Art collections.
3.
Hall-marks.
I. Jones, William Ezelle.
II. Title.

NK7101.L75L674
739.2'3'074019494
76-57976
ISBN 0-87587-077-5

Contents

Acknowledgments

My first thanks must go to Arthur and Rosalinde Gilbert for their generosity and their dedicated collecting. I am grateful to Arthur Grimwade for his assistance and for his catalog essay. Particular gratitude is due Claude Blair and Shirley Bury of the Department of Metalwork, Victoria and Albert Museum, for their courtesy in making their records available to me. Also to Susan Hare, Librarian, The Worshipful Company of Goldsmiths, London, goes my sincere appreciation for sharing both the records and her particular insights regarding the history of that illustrious institution.

My gratitude is extended to John Goodall, F.S.A., for verifying and describing the heraldry on these items, and to John Boyle of the Los Angeles County Department of Weights and Measures for his painstaking care in providing accurate weights for each piece.

I owe the Board of Trustees my thanks for their support of this project. Sincere thanks go to Alla Hall for her extensive research in writing the entries for the Holy Gates (cat. nos. 43 and 44). Patricia Nauert and her staff of the Registrar's Office of the Los Angeles County Museum of Art deserve recognition for their patience and accuracy in measuring and recording these items. I am greatly indebted to Eleanor Hartman, Museum Librarian, and her staff for their unfailing courtesy and assistance, as I am to Syvia Sherwood and Lawrence Margolies, both of the Museum Service Council and the Decorative Arts Council, for their aid in assembling research materials. To Patricia A. Warren, of the Decorative Arts Council, for her assistance in translating mottos and compiling collection data, my sincerest appreciation. As readers will immediately see, this catalog owes much to the beautiful photographs of Ed Cornachio and his staff, John Gebhart and Joe Hazan. For this my thanks.

To Mimi Cohen is due my sincere appreciation for her patience and inestimable assistance in preparing this catalog and helping maintain the Department of Decorative Arts during the production period. I am grateful to Nancy Grubb for her painstaking and excellent editing as well as for her seemingly endless patience.

To Lou Danziger I offer my personal thanks for his unstinting efforts and creative imagination in designing this catalog.

William Ezelle Jones
Curator of Decorative Arts

Preface

The British passion for precious metals wrought by skilled craftsmen was heralded as early as the eighth century by an Anglo-Saxon poet. Although it reached its apogee in the eighteenth and nineteenth centuries, this predilection is still so common that it can be thought of as a national characteristic. It was in this tradition that Arthur and Rosalinde Gilbert were reared in their native England, but it was only after long residence in Los Angeles that they began to acquire wares of silver and gold, not only as gracious pieces for household use, but as *objets de virtù.* To their delight in the beauty of the pieces and their rapidly growing knowledge and connoisseurship they added the kind of discipline that distinguishes the dedicated collector from the dilettante. By avoiding the lure of lesser artisans and sedulously pursuing the works of England's two greatest masters, Paul de Lamerie and Paul Storr—works often monumental in scale in response to royal or aristocratic bidding—the Gilberts were able to assemble in little more than one decade the richest private collection of Georgian silver and the largest of de Lamerie in America.

It was because of their deep love for these splendorous objects that Arthur and Rosalinde Gilbert determined to share them with museum visitors across the country through this exhibition and to make them a permanent legacy to future generations by donating the larger part to the Los Angeles County Museum of Art and bequeathing the remainder. Instead of writing an encomium which even in many pages could only poorly articulate the extent of our gratitude, I should like to express, for all of us, present and future, who will receive such great pleasure from their collection, our simple but deeply earnest thanks to Arthur and Rosalinde Gilbert.

Kenneth Donahue
Director, Los Angeles County Museum of Art

The Gilbert Collection

For their generosity in placing this important collection of English silver on public view Mr. and Mrs. Arthur Gilbert deserve the gratitude of all lovers of the goldsmith's craft—that aspect of the applied arts of England which has a longer continuous history than any other. In concentrating their acquisitions in the work of two great masters—de Lamerie and Storr —they have demonstrated their personal taste and appreciation of the highest levels of design and technique achieved during two of the most outstanding periods in English art, the rococo and the Regency. About three-quarters of a century apart and entirely distinct in inspiration, these works display a parallel recognition by the artists of the magnificent potential of their chosen medium to adorn the houses of their own day and reflect the taste and wealth of their clients.

Paul de Lamerie

De Lamerie dominated the scene of London silver to such an extent that his obituary notice in the London *Evening Post* described him as "particularly famous in making fine ornamental plate, and . . . very instrumental in bringing that Branch of the Trade to the Perfection it is now in." However, when he had first begun working as a newly fledged master he had naturally had to content himself with what simple commissions came his way, and it is not surprising therefore to find that his surviving pieces up to 1720 consist mostly of plain casters, teapots, candlesticks, and so on. But when called upon, he could by 1717 produce such a dignified statement as the covered cup in the collection (cat. no. 1) with its sophisticated open cast straps and palm leaves on body and cover, even though the main form is the standard one then in use by English and Huguenot craftsmen alike. By 1719 de Lamerie was

completely master of the French Regence taste, of which his superb wine cistern now at Minneapolis is perhaps the epitome, although the Gilbert sconces of about 1725 (cat. no. 2) are a worthy challenge to it in their exuberance of design and quality of execution. In the Edgcumbe tureens of 1722 (cat. no. 12) we see the same style of Regence strapwork on the covers but then we are confronted with a curious contradiction of high rococo character in the decoration of the bodies and the handles. Since the asymmetry of the cartouches does not appear elsewhere in de Lamerie's work, or in any other English goldsmith's for that matter, until at least the mid-thirties, one is led to the feeling that the goldsmith was requested by his client to bring the pieces up to date in the latest fashion in about 1735 or so. This view is certainly supported by the way the cover handles span the plain raised circular centers, which seem to be the space originally provided for a central ring handle rising from a molding. If my theory is correct, we have a most interesting and very rare example of de Lamerie's work displaying at one glance the development and variety of his ornamental vocabulary.

The high standard of craftsmanship that de Lamerie's work constantly demonstrates is evident also in the heraldic and decorative engraving of the pieces, which was, of course, a specialized art with its own practitioners. Indeed, in at least one piece— the famous Walpole salver in the Victoria and Albert Museum—we know that de Lamerie employed William Hogarth, who had begun his career by apprenticeship as a silver engraver to the retail goldsmith Ellis Gamble. Two of the pieces in the Gilbert Collection demonstrate distinct styles of the engraver's art: first, the salver or kettle tray of 1726 (cat. no. 3) with its Hogarth-like armorial cartouche and delicate strapwork border, still strictly symmetrical in its design, and secondly, the basket of 1731 (cat. no. 5) with its freely moving design of broken scroll cartouches enclosing scallop shells set at an angle and its broken scroll knots connecting the bordering strapwork, their liveliness echoed by the undulations of the simulated wickerwork of the sides and border. As in other silver forms of the period de Lamerie seems to have been the protagonist of two-handled oval baskets, the earliest of which I have record being a pair of 1724. It was not until about 1738 that he changed to the swing-handled form of which the Gilbert basket of 1741 (cat. no. 15) is an excellent example, with its fine chisel-cut fretwork panels and shellwork set on the amorino mask feet that were to become so characteristic of de Lamerie's work in the last decade of his working life.

We must retrace our steps slightly to consider the first of the imposing trio of teakettles in the collection. The first of these (cat. no. 4), of 1730, is outstanding as an example of how de Lamerie outstripped his contemporaries when called upon to add a new aspect to a standard functional form. Here we have the basic "skittle-ball" kettle of the period enhanced by unusual scale-pattern panels and set on a stand embellished with delightful shell and flambeaux aprons supported by undulating scroll legs resting on shells above which dolphin masks peer out. Of the two kettles of 1736, the example with the fluted, melonlike border (cat. no. 9) is not unlike numerous others by de Lamerie's contemporaries, although naturally displaying the attention to detail and execution that is never missing in this craftsman. The other example with its accompanying circular tray (cat. no. 10) is one of the most superlative of all de Lamerie's productions in this genre. The master touch is immediately apparent in the vigor of the design and modeling of the armorial cartouche with the robust amorino perched above and in the contrasting restraint of the beautifully engraved tray. It should be noted with interest, however, that in spite of the bravura of the whole, the goldsmith was content to use the same model (indeed probably the same mold) for the handle as for that of the simpler kettle of the same year (cat. no. 9). This repeated use of castings in different models can also be demonstrated by the ribbon and floral apron on the stand of the

plainer Gilbert kettle of 1736 which was also used by de Lamerie in another kettle of 1739 (sold in London in 1964), evidence that to some extent silversmiths were in the habit of economizing by reusing existing molds in a new ensemble.

The bravura of the amorino kettle is paralleled by the wonderful pair of sauceboats and stands of 1733 and 1739 (cat. nos. 6–8), in which the boldness of the lion masks on the bodies is echoed by the rippling curves of the handles. The beautiful flat-chased decoration in itself has a secondary function in preventing wear by the feet of the boats, which would inevitably have occurred if the surface had been left plain. It is also interesting to note that the borders of the stands are identical to that of the central oval dish of de Lamerie's great Bobrinskoy centerpiece (1734, Russian State Historical Museum, Moscow), although the chased decoration on that piece is a composition of shells and scrollwork in contrast to the floral nature of the sauceboat stands —another example of the way in which the maker rang the changes in his designs. There is, in my opinion, little doubt that these sauceboats are the finest surviving examples of de Lamerie's rococo expression in this class of object. An added element of their importance is the survival of the original ladles engraved with the Yorke crest, which agrees with the arms of the family engraved on the stands. De Lamerie's inventiveness and constant attention to delicate detail in even such small items is further demonstrated by a smaller pair of ladles of some years later with their scroll and foliage tops (cat. no. 13).

The candlesticks of 1741 (cat. no. 14) show the pleasure the master took in accepting the standard model of the period and enriching it with meticulously finished flowers and shells. Although other makers might well have been capable of producing similar pieces, when one looks, for instance, at the lively little leaves curling down between the shells at the shoulders, one still acknowledges that de Lamerie remains full of individuality and signs his work for the seeing eye in a multitude of unexpected ways.

By 1740 de Lamerie had reached the height of his powers as the master of English rococo silver and it is fitting, therefore, to find in the Gilbert Collection one of his chefs d'oeuvre (cat. no. 17), which challenges comparison with what has long been held to be his masterpiece, the ewer

and dish of the Goldsmiths' Company. While the dish of the latter has perhaps a more sculpturesque quality accentuated by the heavily modeled coat of arms in the center, the ewer of the Gilbert ensemble is in my opinion a more successful exercise, particularly in its gracefully recurving nymph handle as contrasted with the Neptune figure of the Goldsmiths' ewer. The latter leans outwards and results in a loss of balance, both visually and indeed physically, since I know from experience that the slightest touch beneath the ewer's lip sends it falling backwards. Much of the decoration of the dish and the components of the ewer, handle, stem, and foot are castings for which wax models must have first been created. Whether or not de Lamerie was his own modeler we shall probably never know, but it is obvious from comparative studies that all his major pieces of this nature spring from one hand in execution and why should it not have been the goldsmith himself? If we could quote examples in other media of his pouting cherubs' masks, floral festoons, sunbursts, and animated scrolls, we could at least point to a possible artist as the designer or modeler, but as yet no one has appeared as a candidate for the honor.

Of similar virtuosity is the covered cup (cat. no. 18) of the same year as the ewer and dish—1742. Here we must admit in honesty to an *"embarras de richesse"* while not denying the skill of execution. One should note, for instance, the background scenes flanking the amorini or infant bacchanals with the subtle diminution of relief to suggest distance, a technique that links de Lamerie with the great Dutch silversmiths of the seventeenth century—the Vianen brothers and others. Another cup of the same design and year is also recorded by Phillip Phillips in his monograph on de Lamerie, where he describes it as "of the highest decorative effect . . . distinguished in imagination and quality of design and in perfection of execution."

Made for the same noble client as the ewer and dish, Algernon Coote, sixth Earl of Montrath in Ireland, are the fine pair of salvers of 1741–42 (cat. no. 16) with massive borders incorporating masks of the four seasons and grape clusters and with flat-chased floral inner borders similar in quality to those of the sauceboat stands previously described (cat. no. 7). The earl was one of de Lamerie's best clients at this period, for in the same year he also commissioned a pair of cups and covers of equal magnificence and an outstanding epergne. He unfortunately did not live long enough to enjoy their magnificence, dying in 1744, and the silver descended to the Earls of Portarlington, by whom most of the pieces were sold about ninety years ago.

The collection contains no examples of the last nine years of de Lamerie's life, but this is not significant since from the early forties he made little change in style or technique and seems to some extent to have rested on his laurels, content with the fame that was rightly his. Of his powers the present collection speaks with no uncertain voice.

Before we pass on to the achievements of the neoclassical period displayed in this collection we must pause to remark on the basket of 1745 (cat. no. 19), an extremely rare example of the work of Nicholas Sprimont, de Lamerie's contemporary for a short period in the rococo era. Born and trained as a goldsmith in Liège, Belgium, he arrived in London in 1742 and set up in Compton Street. He produced a limited number of highly individual pieces, of which the most remarkable are in the Royal Collection, until he diverted his energies in 1747 to the establishment of the Chelsea porcelain factory. As far as I am aware, the Gilbert basket is the only known piece in this category by Sprimont and in the beautifully modeled masks and wheat ears reflects his skill as no mean rival to the more prolific de Lamerie.

Paul Storr

We turn now to consider the work of Paul Storr, who, it is fair to claim, was the greatest exponent, among all craftsmen of the applied arts, of the neoclassical taste. Naturally enough, Storr's early surviving pieces (like those of de Lamerie) are mostly of a relatively modest functional nature. However, even in 1793, his first year working as a freeman, he was capable of finely executed decorative detail such as Vitruvian scrollwork and anthemion foliage, learned, it seems, from his master Fogelberg. By 1797 he was showing his powers of individual invention in the delightful oval basket of plaited wheat ears (cat. no. 21), of which, as Norman Penzer so aptly said in his monograph on Storr, "the general effect is that of a basket woven in golden corn." In the same year he created one of his most important works,

the gold font for the christening of the Duke of Portland's son. Flanked by figures of Faith, Hope, and Charity, perhaps from designs by John Flaxman, R. A., it offers evidence of the extent to which his reputation had already grown.

From 1800 onwards Storr made himself master of the classical taste in a wide range of designs and objects, even when these were basically utilitarian, such as his kettle of 1802 (cat. no. 22) or his hot water jug or coffeepot of seven years later (cat. no. 25). Each has curved claw supports topped by pendant rings adapted from the stems of Roman tripods and double serpent handles in a combination of silver and ivory. The kettle has interesting affinities to another of the same year, formerly in the collection of the Duke of Manchester, with a similar handle and diagonal fluted band but with a calyx of palm leaves below and set on a low circular stand with winged paw feet. The jug also resembles one of 1805 with a plain wooden handle, now in the Fairhaven collection.

The eclectic way in which Storr conceived his designs is admirably illustrated by the most important items in the Gilbert Collection, the two pairs of soup tureens of 1806 (cat. no. 23). With their strange blend of Egyptian sphinx and winged Diana of Ephesus handles, they are closely related to four gilt examples of 1805 in the English Royal Collection, which have, as a difference, sphinxes flanking the bases instead of the hinged lions present in the Gilbert examples. The circular stands of both sets are derived, as E. Alfred Jones has shown in *The Gold and Silver of Windsor Castle,* from a pair of Louis XVI tureens by Henri Auguste of 1787, also in the Royal Collection. The connection with the royal tureens is emphasized by the fact that the Gilbert examples came originally from the collection of Ernest, Duke of Cumberland, one of George III's sons, who became King of Hanover after the accession to the English throne of Queen Victoria in 1837. It was then that large quantities of English silver kept in Hanover by the Georgian sovereigns passed with the Hanoverian Crown, to be dispersed eventually in London in 1924.

The scope of entertaining in the great houses of the day which created such a large market for Storr's magnificent conceptions is admirably illustrated by the magnificent gilt tray of 1808 (cat. no. 24), over a yard in overall length. That the

masks adjoining the handles are related to "Comic and tragic masks of Silenus" illustrated in Thomas Hope's *Household Furniture and Interior Decoration* (1807) is a further example of Storr's ability and quickness to make use of the latest of other men's designs. Massiveness in plate design, which one writer of the day considered the most desirable feature, is particularly emphasized by the stately urn of 1809 (cat. no. 25), with its strongly modeled Imperial Roman features of lion masks and paw feet. A lighter note of the same inspiration is struck by the beautifully modeled caryatids of the dessert stand of 1810 (cat. no. 26), although it may perhaps be thought that the swags of naturalistic fruit draping the plinth and the large bearded masks are somewhat out of key with the former. Another pair of these stands of the same year, but supporting circular plaited baskets, are in the Wellington Museum, London, and centerpieces of 1811 and 1812 have survived as further examples of the requirements for the large banquet tables of the day.

Another classical feature much used by Storr was the baluster tripod candelabrum decorated with acanthus, which is known in various marble versions. This can be seen as the main element in the centerpiece of 1813 (cat. no. 27) with its triangular plinth flanked by three very British-looking lions and in the pair of elegant candelabra of 1816 (cat. no. 32), of which the lowest stage of the acanthus foliage and the in-curved plinths appear to be the same model as the preceding. Of all classical forms in the Regency period the famous vase acquired by the Earl of Warwick in 1774 was the most popular. It is only fitting, therefore, that the present collection should contain an example of 1814 (cat. no. 28), suitably mounted on a well-proportioned pedestal engraved with a grandiloquent inscription and the arms of the recipient. The vase was, we might well say, the "best-seller" of its day, allowing the goldsmith to reuse the original model and molds for further commissions and thus increase his profits by reducing his preparatory costs.

We catch another glimpse of Storr's eclectic use of design in the set of candlesticks of 1815 (cat. no. 30), which are identical to a pair of one year earlier, from the Cumberland-Hanover collection and now in the Victoria and Albert Museum. The lowest section of the stem, resembling a many-petaled upturned flower, is the same as in a pair of candelabra by the same maker of 1807, formerly at Woburn Abbey, seat of the Dukes of Bedford. Storr had modeled the latter on a set of George II candlesticks by the Huguenot goldsmith Paul Crespin, also in the Bedford family collection. We thus have a further example of the way in which this accomplished master could plagiarize his own earlier work and at the same time achieve a new and thoroughly satisfying entity. It will of course be noted that in these candlesticks of 1815 we have virtually no classical influence and that the basic effect is of a return to the richly loaded decorative detail of the French Regence taste in the stems merging with a revival of rococo motifs in the bases to result in an opulent display of the richest Regency style.

Much the same effect is achieved in the imposing covered entree dishes of 1816–17 (cat. no. 33), the covers loaded with festoons of fruit and flowers interspersed with blossomed trellis panels, parted to allow space for the proud owner's coat of arms. Who would not feel his gastric juices stimulated by this magnificence to do full justice to the rich viands concealed within? And when the feast was over what better implement to use in ladling out the steaming punch than the gracefully curving shell-bowled ladle also to be seen in the collection (cat. no. 29)? This magnificence for the table was reflected by Storr in even such minor pieces as the cruet and soy frames of 1816 (cat. no. 31), with their sharply cut crystal glass bottles enriched with silver acanthus necks and set in elaborately chased stands. What an age of leisured opulence supported by ranks of liveried servants is conjured up for us as we consider these lesser products of the master's workshop. As a coda to this Storr symphony we have the delightful covered glass bowl of 1820 (cat. no. 34) with its vine and ivy festoons, of which the original purpose seems somewhat obscure but which was perhaps an ice container or a compote bowl.

Benjamin Smith and His Firm

Storr's representation in the Gilbert Collection is balanced by five fine items from the workshop of his rival suppliers to Rundell and Bridge, the royal goldsmiths. This was the firm that commenced working at Greenwich in 1802 as a partnership of Digby Scott and Benjamin Smith, the latter, and almost certainly the former, having previously worked for Matthew Boulton in Birmingham. In 1807 Smith entered a separate mark alone and then in 1809 another in partnership with his brother James, followed by two separate marks in 1812 and 1814 and then one in 1816 with his son Benjamin, who worked with him until 1818, after which father and son went their separate ways. From the start this varying partnership, of which Benjamin Smith the senior seems to have been the dominant personality, equaled Storr in the quality of their productions. Their most important work is probably the extensive Jamaica service in the Royal Collection and they are notable too for their magnificent vine-bordered trays and dessert stands, of which the oval tray of 1805 (cat. no. 35) and the beautiful engraved stands of 1808–10 (cat. no. 37) in the collection are outstanding examples. The Egyptian-style candelabra of 1806 (cat. no. 36) and the imposing wine coolers of 1811 (cat. no. 38) lose nothing in comparison with similar essays by Storr. Although unfortunately no records have survived to show how Rundell and Bridge apportioned the orders they received between Storr and the Smith establishment, the amount of work that has survived from the two firms seems to indicate that Storr's output, and hence by argument the working strength of his establishment, was the larger. In spite of its entirely different genre, the fine vase-shaped ewer by Benjamin Smith III of 1834 (cat. no. 39) shows no relaxation in technical quality.

Royal and Other Silver

The remaining pieces of the Gilbert Collection are varied both in nature and country of origin. Among the English silver, pride of place must be given to the imposing wine cistern of 1794 (cat. no. 20) by James and Elizabeth Bland. This bears the arms of, and was made for, Augustus Frederick, Duke of Sussex, sixth son of George III, a prince of wide culture and liberal outlook. He displayed considerable taste for silver collecting, and after his death in 1843 his collection was sold at Christie's, the sale taking four days. The wine cistern used for cooling a quantity of bottles suggests that his liking for conviviality equaled his other activities. Next to that made for his brother, the Duke of York, it is the last but one in the long line of these large vessels, which stretches from the time of Charles II onwards and has no parallel in the surviving silver of any other country. The makers were the son and widow of Cornelius Bland (who had been apprenticed in 1761) but other than this massive piece they are known for little more than simple plain domestic pieces. It seems curious that they should have been capable of producing the wine cistern, but since their workshop was in Bunhill Row—outside the boundaries of the old city of London and certainly not an area for important retail shops—their mark on the cistern must indicate production rather than retail sponsorship of another's work.

Another item in the collection with English royal origins is the delightful and unique set of candlesticks decorated with "Chinamen" and drinking figures (cat. no. 40). The last item of royal silver in the collection is the pair of rare pilgrim bottles of 1825 (cat. no. 41) engraved with both the arms of another of George III's sons, Frederick, Duke of York, and those of the Marquess of Cleveland, into whose collection they passed after the former's death and sale at Christie's in 1827. These are by one of the more unusual London silversmiths of the George IV period, Edward Farrell, who worked mainly to the order of a successful retailer, Kensington Lewis of St. James's Street, and who supplied a number of large and heavily ornamented pieces to his royal customer. Of a similar highly decorative nature is the pair of early Victorian wine coasters (cat. no. 42) by Robert Garrard, who succeeded his father in 1818 and was appointed as royal goldsmith in 1830.

The two superb pairs of Russian Royal Gates (cat. nos. 43, 44) from two Kiev churches dating from 1784 provide further evidence of Mr. and Mrs. Gilbert's appreciation of richness of design and the highest quality of execution of which the silver craftsman is capable.

Arthur Grimwade, F. S. A.

Silversmithing Techniques

In its pure form silver, like gold, is too soft to withstand the wear of everyday use, and from classical times silversmiths have alloyed silver with other metals for strength and hardness.[1] Copper has proven the most satisfactory alloy in providing the needed durability without changing the appearance or the malleability of silver. In 1238 the first known law was passed in Britain prescribing the proportion of 925 parts silver to 75 parts copper. This ratio, **Sterling Standard** eventually called the Sterling Standard,[2] applied to both coins and silver domestic objects and has been kept constant by government control ever since. This surveillance has maintained reliable standards of silver for seven hundred years.

From September 26, 1300 (during the reign of Edward I), hallmarks have been legally required as proof of government assay. No piece of silver "was to depart out of the hands of the workers" without having been assayed and certified with the assayer's mark. The leopard head, formerly the private ensign for the king, was adopted to signify London as the City of Assay. Other symbols were later adopted as assay offices were created around the country. Beginning in 1478 the Goldsmiths' Company required that every piece be stamped with a letter date. The letters (only twenty were used originally) were changed on the 19th of May (St. Dunstan's Day) each year, thereby identifying the term of office of each assayer should the silver quality be questioned. The lion passant gardant (looking over the left shoulder) was added in 1544 as a symbol for sterling and was replaced in London after 1821 with the lion passant (looking straight ahead).

With the civil wars of the mid-seventeenth century, domestic and royal plate was melted down to produce coins to pay the mounting war debts. Later, Cromwellian austerity discouraged displays of wealth and kept many family sideboards bare till the restoration of Charles II, when a revived desire for pomp was satisfied with lavish new plate. As a result, the earlier process was reversed, and coins became scarce as they were melted down to produce plate. This shortage of coins and the Crown's financial troubles eventually resulted in the Act of Parliament, 1697, which increased the purity of silver to be used in wrought items. (To eliminate the problem of "clipping"[3] other regulations required for the first time that coins be regularly shaped with milled edges.) The ratio of silver to alloy metal was raised from 925 parts per 1,000 to 953.3 parts of silver, or 11 oz., 10 dwt. per troy pound. This higher standard required all new hallmarks to **Britannia Standard** distinguish it from sterling. Maker's marks were changed from the silversmith's initials to the first two letters of his last name. The lion passant gardant for the Sterling Standard was replaced by a representation of Britannia, which gave the standard its common name—*Britannia Standard*. Replacing the crowned leopard head for the London assay office was a new stamp of a lion head erased (with an irregular neck edge). Along with these new marks a new series of letter dates began in March 1697. During the twenty-three years that the Britannia Standard was enforced, it achieved the desired effect of keeping coins in circulation. The return to the Sterling Standard on 1 June 1720 did not abolish use of the more expensive silver; the regulation permitted silversmiths who preferred and could afford the softer alloy to continue using it. Paul de Lamerie was obviously one who did not worry about the added expense, for he used Britannia

---

1. D. E. Strong, *Greek and Roman Gold and Silver Plate*, Ithaca: Cornell University Press, 1966, p. 4.
2. Though the origins of the word *sterling* are lost, it probably derives from *easterlings*, the name for the East German coin makers brought to England by Henry II to improve his domestic coinage.
3. The unscrupulous would literally clip corners and edges from the flat, irregularly shaped coins, reducing their weight and value.

silver exclusively for the next twelve years, finally registering a new sterling mark with the Goldsmiths' Company in 1732.

Preparation

Until the nineteenth century, silver was extracted from raw ore by a process known as *leaching,* in which all base metals were removed by nitric acid, leaving only the pure silver. This silver was then alloyed with the appropriate percentage of copper and cast into ingots. Even though rolling mills had begun producing stock sheet silver as early as the late seventeenth century, silversmiths generally hammered the ingots into sheets themselves throughout most of the eighteenth century.

Raising

To produce a bowl, teakettle, tureen, or other vessel from sheet silver the silversmith first estimated the amount of silver needed and worked it flat, then cut a circle from the sheet. Placing the circle of silver over a shallow depression in a ridged wood block, he hammered around the shape with a ball peen hammer, starting at the outer edge and spiraling in to the center, until a saucer shape was produced. By repeating this process and varying the shape of the depression the silversmith could produce a flaring bowl or basket. By working the silver over a narrow rounded anvil, he could produce a "skittleball"– shaped teakettle. Every effort was made to keep the walls of a raised piece even by hammering carefully in regular patterns, but most rounded pieces needed to be turned on a lathe for final evening of the visible surface. Any remaining unevenness was disguised under chased decorations.

Annealing

Because hammering distorted the crystal structure of the silver, annealing was necessary to restore the resilience of the metal before it could be rehammered. The object was placed on a pan called a *hearth* which was heated red hot, and then the silver was "quenched" in cold water. The silversmith has traditionally determined the point at which the silver is ready for quenching by the color it turns in the heating process. The repeated hammering, heating, and cooling, though painstaking and time consuming, strengthened the silver.

Casting

Handles, feet, spouts, and applied deco- ration were cast of molten silver, generally in molds purchased from mold makers, although a few silversmiths like de Lamerie made their own. From an original usually carved in wood or metal, molds were produced in marl, a special casting sand held in a rigid metal case divided in half. After being dried and pressed together, the molds were filled with molten silver. Once the silver cast cooled, it required cleaning and refining to improve surface details.

Soldering

Cast parts were joined to the other parts with a solder that had to be at least Sterling Standard and have the same melting point as the elements to be joined. Because the parts had to be heated over charcoal, controlling the temperature for the joining was extremely difficult. The brass-alloy solder of the eighteenth century had a higher melting point and slightly different color than today's zinc-alloy solder.

Chasing

The creation of surface textures and patterns, as well as the removal of ragged edges and mold marks from newly cast or soldered pieces, was generally achieved by chasing. No metal is lost in this technique; the silver is merely moved around by hammering the surface with hard metal punches and other devices.

Engraving

Flat surfaces like those on trays, basins, and cups were decorated with engraving, in which the silver was actually cut away[4] to produce a pattern or design. Engraving grew so popular that silversmiths often employed full-time engravers in their workshops.[5] Over the years engraving styles changed as much as the silver they embellished. For example, large heraldic representations engraved in the center of trays were not fashionable in the early 1800s, but later in the century they became so prevalent that today it is hard to envision that form without heraldry.

Polishing

A broad-faced hammer called a *planisher* was used to remove surface irregularities before various grades of abrasives were rubbed on to smooth any uneven spots and produce a deep, lustrous shine. Finally, jewelers' rouge was applied, frequently with the heel of the hand or the forearm for a softer polish.

Fire Gilding

The procedure followed in the eighteenth and early nineteenth centuries to make silver items appear gold is known as fire gilding. Grains of gold were heated red hot then thrown into heated mercury and mixed till blended. When cooled, the mixture formed a yellowish mass with the consistency of butter. This amalgam was then ready to be applied to the finished silver piece, which had been bathed in nitric acid and mercury to help effect the bond. The gold mixture was spread evenly over the prepared surface and carefully heated to burn off the mercury. The resulting surface was a dull yellow, which was next covered with gilding wax—beeswax mixed with either red ocher, copper scale, alum, or borax—then fired again to heighten the color and remove any residual mercury. The extensive use of mercury in this process was extremely dangerous, and many of the workmen who used it were eventually inflicted with a form of mercury poisoning, also known as "Mad Hatter's disease." The nineteenth-century invention of electro-plating eliminated fire gilding from common practice.[6]

Just as government assaying has maintained the standards of English silver, so control by The Worshipful Company of Goldsmiths has maintained the quality of craftsmanship. An extension of the medieval guild, the Company regulated the apprenticeship system and maintained the records that make English silversmithing one of the best documented arts in the world. Traditionally, each applicant to the Company was required to serve for seven years under a master silversmith to whom he was bound by a contract held at Goldsmiths' Hall. The master's tutelage covered each aspect of the silversmith's art, from model making to the final polishing. These apprentices were usually the only assistants in the master's shop and served as his extra hands. Once the apprenticeship had been served the apprentice was required to make his "masterpiece," an object of his choosing to be submitted to the company masters for approval before he could be granted his registered mark. This system

4. By the mid-nineteenth century acid-etched engraving was fairly widely used.
5. Clayton, p. 119.
6. *Encyclopedia Britannica,* Chicago, 1958, vol. X, p. 349. For further information on silversmithing techniques see Clayton, pp. 257–61, which was the source for much of this material.

changed little over the centuries until the Industrial Revolution made it obsolete.

With the rise of the Sheffield plate industry, relatively low-cost silver items became available for a burgeoning middle-class market. (Sheffield plate has a copper core sandwiched between sheets of silver, all hammered together to create a single sheet. The use of copper significantly diminished the amount of silver required and thus reduced costs). As a result, silversmiths lost many of the small "bread and butter" commissions they had previously relied on, and had to adopt new marketing techniques. The history of Rundell, Bridge & Rundell exemplifies this transition from a small silversmith shop to a vast business employing more than three hundred workers and producing massive services and presentation pieces. The resulting compartmentalization of responsibilities and a shift to company control of maker's marks, coupled with the invention of electroplating, effectively ended the silversmithing tradition in all but a few workshops until the surge of renewed interest with the rise of the crafts tradition in the second half of the nineteenth century.

William Ezelle Jones

William Hogarth
English, 1697–1764
The Rake's Progress, Plate I (of six), 1735
Engraving
14 x 16½ in. (35 x 41.9 cm.)
Los Angeles County Museum of Art
The Paul Rodman Mabury Collection
m. 46. 5. 2

Catalog

Paul Jacques de Lamerie   English, 1688–1751

Born to Huguenot parents—9 April 1688

Baptized at 's Hertogenbosch (Bois-le-Duc), Holland—14 April 1688

Brought to England—March 1689

To London—1691

Apprenticed to Peter Plattel (born Pierre Platel)—6 August 1703

Freed from apprenticeship—4 February 1713

First mark entered (Britannia Standard), Windmill Street, St. James's, London— 5 February 1713

Goldsmith to the King—1716

Admitted to livery of Worshipful Company of Goldsmiths, London—18 July 1717

Second mark entered (Sterling Standard), Windmill Street—17 March 1733

Moved to 45 Gerrard Street, London—1738

Third mark entered (Sterling Standard), Windmill Street—27 June 1739

Elected Fourth Warden, Company of Goldsmiths—1743

Elected Third Warden—1746

Elected Second Warden (never elected Prime Warden, possibly due to ill health)—1747

Died in London—1 August 1751

---

1. **Two-Handled Covered Cup,** 1717

Height: 11⅜ in. (28.9 cm.)
Width: 11¼ in. (28.6 cm.)
Diameter of lip: 6½ in. (16.5 cm.)
Diameter of base: 5⁷/₁₆ in. (13.9 cm.)
Diameter of lid: 6⅝ in. (16.9 cm.)
Total weight: 76 oz., 16 dwt. (2,388.403 grams)
m. 75.135.43a,b

Form

The tall two-handled covered cup evolved from the low porringer or caudle cup, reaching its greatest height in about 1775. In the eighteenth century, as today, these cups were presentation pieces and prized family status symbols.[1]

The popularity of these cups rose with the influx of Huguenot silversmiths into England during the last decades of the seventeenth century, for the French refugees found the tall cup a particularly receptive form on which to exercise their decorative techniques. At the same time, they and their English counterparts produced a simpler version, probably of Dutch origin, that was devoid of applied decoration. De Lamerie produced cups in both styles throughout his career.[2]

Although the shape of the cup bowl changed little throughout the eighteenth century, the handle design progressed from the simple S-curve, seen on this cup, to the later, more elaborate double-C-scroll handle.

Hallmarks

De Lamerie's first mark.

Lion head erased and Britannia (both for Britannia Standard).

Capital B (letter date for 1717).

Struck outside on plain upper band on back of cup near juncture with handle and again inside lid near rim.

Engraved Arms

Herbert impaling Smith of London, with crest of Herbert.

Party Azure and Gules, three lions rampant Or (Herbert).

Impaling Azure two bars between three broad arrows Or (Smith of London).

On a wreath a wyvern (crest of Herbert).

Marriage unidentified.

The body of this presentation-scale cup is bound (for strength as well as decoration) with a cast rim and band at mid-body. The S-scroll handles are cast from the molds that de Lamerie used only in the second decade of the century (note the distinctive wedge-shaped "cushions" at the top joint of the handle, which are characteristic of his early style). In developing his rococo style of the 1740s, de Lamerie created particularly inventive handle designs to harmonize with his elaborate rococo surface decorations (see cat. no. 18).

The applied decorative devices at the bottom curve of the bowl and on the low dome of the lid are derived from a cut-card technique but are realized here in finely chased low relief on a textured mat background.[3] The leaf motif on the handles is repeated along the outer rim of the two-hipped base, while the inner rim echoes in chased form the strapwork pattern of the applied and engraved lambrequins.

Unlike most London silversmiths, who bought their molds from common mold makers, de Lamerie is believed to have designed and produced his own molds for handles, finials, and applied decorations. Though he used the same cast parts on several of his works, they are characteristically his designs and not identical to other silversmiths' molded parts.[4]

1. Clayton, p. 94.
2. Hayward, p. 8.
3. Clayton, p. 96.
4. Ibid., p. 174.

2. **Pair of Two-Light Sconces,** ca. 1725

Silver gilt
Height: 22⅛ in. (56.2 cm.)
Backplate width: 4⅞ in. (12.4 cm.)
Reach of arms: 9⅜ in. (23.9 cm.)
Wax pan diameter: 4¾ in. (12 cm.)
Total weight: 229 oz. (7,122.686 grams)
1: 113 oz., 5 dwt. (3,522.363 grams)
2: 115 oz., 15 dwt. (3,600.323 grams)
m. 77.2.1a,b

Hallmarks

De Lamerie's first mark (struck three times on each).

Crowned leopard head (London assay).

1: Scratch engraved on back 111–16 and 109 (for weight).

2: Scratch engraved on back 108–16 and 108.7 (for weight).

Struck on the back of the backplates.

Cast and Chased Arms

Argent a fess engrailed between three cinquefoils in a border Sable.

A baron's coronet above.

For Thomas Foley, created Baron Foley of Kidderminster in 1712 (d. 1733).

Form

Sconces, or wall lights, were developed as devices to intensify candlelight with reflective surfaces. The earliest surviving silver sconces date from the late seventeenth century and hold either a single candle in a galleried tray below a long embossed surface or candles in one or more scrolled branches that spring from large oval embossed plaques. When not made of mirrored glass, backplates were frequently made of extremely thin silver to minimize expense.

Royal inventories of the 1600s and 1700s indicate the variety of these popular fixtures used to light the interiors of palaces and country houses.[1] Few still exist, a scarcity due in part to changing lighting techniques and to the reworking of silver, but also to the fragile nature of most sconce construction.[2] With the Huguenot influence during the second half of the seventeenth century, English sconces were improved markedly by the addition of solid cast backplates and branches.

The slender cast backplate with scrolling branches—a form popular in the first decade of the eighteenth century—indicates the shift in emphasis from reflective to decorative qualities as sconces became less popular. By 1725 sconces had apparently ceased to be the prevalent source of interior lighting.[3] No reason for this eclipse is known other than a preference for the portability of candlesticks and the new multi-branched candelabra.

Unique in de Lamerie's work, this pair of silver-gilt sconces ranks with his three or four greatest works. By achieving a sound solution to a difficult structural problem and utilizing construction elements as a basis for a complex decorative scheme, he created sconces that transcend their utilitarian function.

The slender backplates are cast in three parts. Their bold moldings add strong horizontal emphasis to the vertical shape, while also concealing the pinned and soldered joints of the three cast sections and providing maximum strength. The horizontal joint of the bottom two sections provides substantial mass for securing and supporting the heavy cast S-scroll branches and large cast wax pans. De Lamerie created strong horizontal emphasis even on the branches of the sconces with the square capitals beneath the wax pans and the curious brackets that effectively break the S-curve of the branches.

The decorative surfaces of the plates are surmounted with baron's coronets in the style of slender sconces of the 1700s, but there the similarity ends. De Lamerie created on these backplates a vertical succession of decorative motifs, separated into panels by the pronounced horizontal moldings, but edged with repeated and continuous scrolls and strapwork. On the bottom third of the composition—that area of the sconces receiving the least direct light and therefore the least visible—de Lamerie used low-relief strapwork on a mat surface. On the upper two-thirds—where flickering candlelight creates the greatest dramatic effect—he used high-relief scrolling brackets and exotic human masks.

The absence of complete hallmarks indicates that de Lamerie created these sconces from reclaimed Britannia silver, which had already been worked, assayed, and taxed.

1. Hayward, p. 63. Inventories of 1721 indicate that at St. James's Palace there were twenty-eight silver sconces, fourteen large mirrored sconces, and ten picture sconces (with embossed pictorial backplates); at Kensington Palace, twenty-four sconces of various types; at Hampton Court, eighteen; and at Windsor, fifty.
2. Oman, 1934, p. 174.
3. Grimwade, 1974, p. 57.

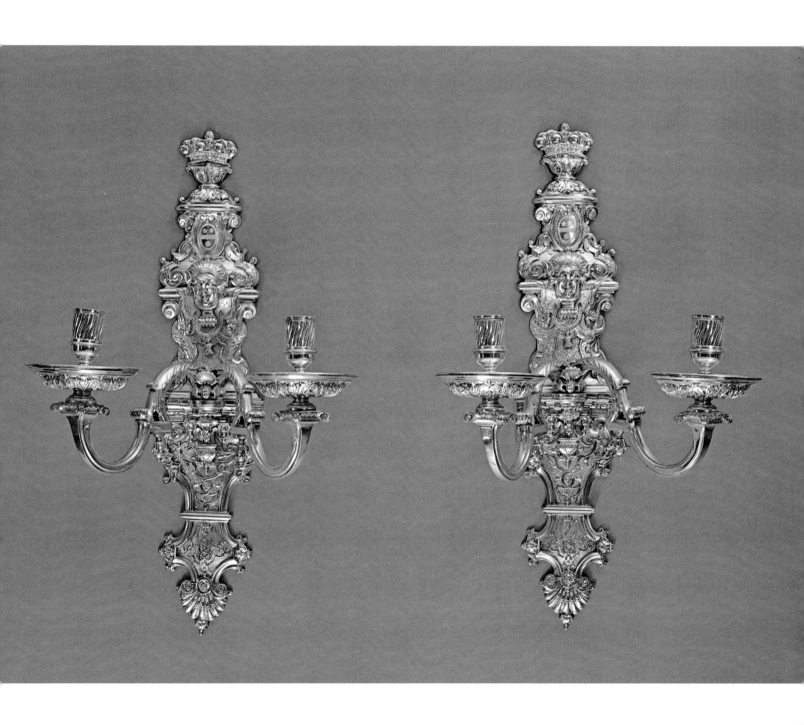

3. Strawberry Dish, 1726

Height: 1⅝ in. (4.2 cm.)
Diameter: 13 in. (33 cm.)
Total weight: 28 oz., 9 dwt.
(885.906 grams)
m. 77.2.22

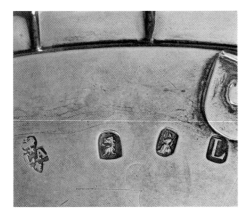

Hallmarks

De Lamerie's first mark.

Lion head erased and Britannia (both for Britannia Standard).

Capital *L* (letter date for 1726).

Struck on underside near edge.

Engraved Arms

A chevron between three crescents.

Impaling a lion rampant in a border engrailed.

All in an elaborate cartouche.

Engraving contemporary with manufacture but omission of tinctures (conventional hatching to represent heraldic colors) from the engraved arms makes certain identification impossible.

Form

One of the simplest dish constructions, the strawberry dish is formed from a single sheet of silver, with only the three feet made from added metal. After the round outer surface of the dish is drawn upward by hammering, the edge is crimped into characteristic fluting, giving the thin silver added strength from the resulting compound curves. A scalloped outer rim adds to the decorative appearance. Although "strawberry dish" is the currently accepted term for this smaller version of the salver, it indicates only one of several uses for these dishes. Larger versions with deeper sides are referred to as salad dishes, while smaller ones are known to have served as spoon trays. The serviceable size and the simple construction with minimal use of the metal and generous space for decorative engraving made the strawberry dish a popular addition to domestic plate of the eighteenth century.

This large strawberry dish illustrates the craftsmanship that de Lamerie achieved early in his career. Most characteristic of his later style is the delicacy of the engraved inner border and of the cartouche encircling the arms. Based on seventeenth-century French decorative borders, the engraving is more sophisticated than the modest form it decorates, but de Lamerie has achieved a balance between the simple, unadorned surface and the contained small-scale engraved detail that elevates this piece above its more mundane counterparts.

4. Kettle on Stand, 1730

Extreme height: 12½ in. (31.8 cm.)
Extreme width: 8 in. (20.3 cm.)
Kettle height: 8¾ in. (22.2 cm.)
Kettle diameter: 6½ in. (16.5 cm.)
Stand height: 4¼ in. (10.8 cm.)
Stand diameter: 5¼ in. (13.3 cm.)
Total weight: 70 oz., 1 dwt.
(2,179.329 grams)
Kettle: 35 oz., 3 dwt. (1,093.208 grams)
Stand: 34 oz., 18 dwt. (1,086.121 grams)
m. 77.2.23a,b

Hallmarks

De Lamerie's first mark.

Lion head erased and Britannia (both for Britannia Standard).

Capital *P* (letter date for 1730).

Struck inside applied rim on bottom of kettle only.

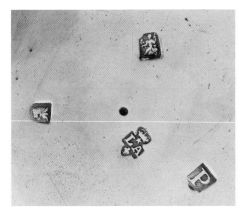

Form

With the increasing popularity of tea in England during the late seventeenth and eighteenth centuries, special utensils for storing, preparing, and serving the new beverage proliferated. Teapots[1] remained small, reflecting the high cost of tea,[2] and their small size required frequent replenishing of hot water. To answer this need, the metal kettle on a burner-equipped stand was devised. The first is recorded in 1679 as "one Indian furnac [*sic*] for tea" in the inventories of Ham House, Richmond; the earliest surviving example is at Norwich Castle Museum,[3] which dates from 1694. These kettles on stands are usually pear-shaped with swing handles at top, resting on a four-legged (later three-legged) stand with burner.

This is the earliest of the three pumpkin-shaped kettles on stands in the Gilbert Collection that illustrate the evolution of de Lamerie's rococo style.

The body of this kettle is divided vertically by spinelike bands alternating with panels of overlapping scales that increase in size from top to bottom. The scale motif is repeated on the burner pan, the scroll of the three-legged stand, and in bands on the blunt spout. This kettle and a lantern-shaped coffeepot, decorated with the same motifs and dating from 1731,[4] are seemingly unique examples in de Lamerie's oeuvre of compositions in a mannerist style.[5] The absence of any similarly decorated pieces indicates that de Lamerie's revival of the earlier mannerist style met with no popular success. This kettle on stand, however, heralds the beginning of his exploration in unusual directions for a personal decorative style. By mid-decade these efforts became recognizable as his own rococo style.

De Lamerie's probable source of inspiration was the work of Christian Van Vianen (1598–1666 or later), a Dutch silversmith who had applied the "auricular" or "cartilaginous" decorative style to his silver a century earlier.[6] Engravings of the seventeenth century reveal an abundance of similar devices.

1. Teapots, for the brewing of tea, generically have fixed handles at the side opposite the spout.
2. Oman, 1934, p. 151. The small size of ceramic teapots also reflected the limits caused by production problems in the burgeoning ceramic industry.
3. Ibid.
4. Phillips, p. 91, pl. LXVIII.
5. The late sixteenth- and seventeenth-century mannerist style was a deliberate contradiction of the classical vocabulary and orderliness of the Renaissance. De Lamerie's efforts at mannerism can be considered a direct reaction to the conservatism of English taste in silver.
6. Clayton, p. 331.

De Lamerie

5. Two-Handled Basket, 1731

Height: 4 in. (10.2 cm.)
Extreme length: 14¾ in. (37.5 cm.)
Basket length: 13 in. (33 cm.)
Width: 11 in. (28 cm.)
Total weight: 57 oz., 4 dwt.
(1,778.90 grams)
m. 75. 135.49

Hallmarks

De Lamerie's first mark.

Lion head erased and Britannia (both for Britannia Standard).

Capital *Q* (indistinct) (letter date for 1731).

Struck on bottom near center.

Scratch engraved 58−9 (for weight).

Engraved Arms

Walpole impaling Shorter with a Garter.

The supporters[1] and motto of the Earl of Orford, for Sir Robert Walpole K. G. Or on a fess between two chevrons Sable three cross crosslets Or (Walpole).

Sable a lion rampant Or crowned Argent between three axes Argent handles Or (Shorter).

All within the Garter.

Supporters: an antelope and stag Argent attired Proper collared checky Or and Azure, chained Or.

Motto: *Fari quae sentiat* ("He speaks what he thinks").

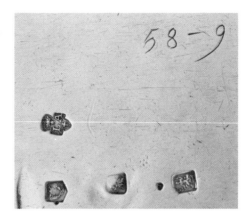

Form

Appearing first in a circular shape, the silver table basket with pierced sides made its debut at the end of the sixteenth century. Called variously a table, bread, cake, or dessert basket, this useful form is known to have served as a sewing basket as well. By the eighteenth century the basket was most popular in an oval shape with pierced and chased sides worked to resemble baskets woven of osier or wicker. Though such baskets were handleless at first, by the beginning of the 1700s D-hoop handles were applied at the ends. De Lamerie produced a number of these popular baskets in the 1730s, all with similar design features[2] and fine engraving. By 1734 he was already producing a new version of this basket with a single-hinged wing handle.[3]

1. The engraving illustrates the numerous errors that can occur in heraldic application. Robert Walpole, created Knight of the Garter 26 May 1726, was not created Earl of Orford until 6 February 1742. No evidence can be found that he was granted supporters (here present) with his peerage (these are commonly granted when an individual is created an earl). The engraving here appears original with the manufacture of the basket in 1731. A further misapplication is the enclosure of the combined arms of the knight and wife. The Garter is intended for the knight alone.
2. Phillips. pls. LXXIII–LXXVI, p. 92.
3. Clayton, ill. 12, p. 22.

De Lamerie

The sides and the oval bottom of this basket are formed from separate sheets of silver. Once shaped, the basket was pierced to produce the effect of open basketwork and then chased to create the illusion of woven reeds. The sides and foot ring are soldered to the bottom at right angles and reinforced with cast rings of bound reeding. The pierced, chased sides lift and flare from the base, extending out to form the undulating scalloped lip. A cast half-round band of bound reeding is applied inside the lip at the shoulder. Over this is applied a decorative band of twisted wire that repeats the twisted-wire treatment of the outer edge. Twin handles made of twisted wire and rope-twined strands are formed into D-hoop handles and attached to the upright sides at each end of the basket. A diapered pattern is flat engraved on the bottom of the basket, surrounding the central oval containing the engraved arms.

6. Boats, 1733

1: Extreme height: 4¾ in. (12.1 cm.)
Extreme length: 9½ in. (24.1 cm.)
Width: $4^9/_{16}$ in. (11.6 cm.)
2: Extreme height: $4^{11}/_{16}$ in. (12. cm.)
Extreme length: $9^9/_{16}$ in. (24.3 cm.)
Width: $4^9/_{16}$ in. (11.6 cm.)
Total weight: 47 oz., 12 dwt.
(1,479.464 grams)
1: 24 oz., 1 dwt. (747.705 grams)
2: 23 oz., 11 dwt. (731.759 grams)
m. 77.2. 2a, b

Form

Pairs of sauceboats were one of the many table service innovations during the reign of George I. Created first in double-lipped form with handles at either side and raised on a single flared foot, sauceboats began to appear about 1719. This form continued to be made, though with diminishing popularity, until the 1730s. Single-lip boats appeared about 1726 and from that time on became the most popular shape in silver.[1] The popularity of sauces and of the boats to serve them at table caused sets of four, six, and even eight to be made, and exceptional services required stands for each boat.

Hallmarks

De Lamerie's second mark.

Lion passant gardant (Sterling Standard).

Crowned leopard head (London assay).

Capital S (letter date for 1733).

Struck on center bottoms.

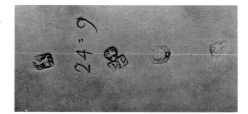

Engraved Arms

Quarterly Yorke, Meller, and Hutton (?), in pretense the arms of Wynne, the crest of Yorke for Phillip Yorke of Erddig, Denbighshire, married Diana Wynne in 1782 and died in 1804.

Quarterly 1 and 4, Argent on a saltire Azure a bezant (Yorke).

2, Argent three blackbirds a chief indented Sable (Meller).

3, Gules a fess Or between three lozenge-shaped cushions each charged with a roundel (cf. Hutton).

Over all a scocheon Gules a Saracen's head erased Proper wreathed about the temples Argent and Sable (Wynne).

On a wreath, a lion's head erased Proper collared (Gules thereon a bezant) (crest of Yorke).

The arms added a generation after manufacture of boats.

---

1. Double-lipped boats were produced as late as 1755 in England's new soft paste porcelain at the Dr. Wall Factory, Worcester. But these examples produced in ceramics were all deliberate attempts to gain the prestige of established silver forms for the products of this new, somewhat uncertain, industry.

The slightly rounded bodies of these low oval boats are each raised from one piece of silver, with the sides worked into smoothly flaring rims that rise at one end to form high-lipped spouts. Each body is supported by four applied, identically cast, large lion masks on short legs with paw feet. This lion mask and leg combination was popular with London silversmiths in the 1730s and continued in use into the 1750s. Between the lion masks on the sides of the bodies are applied cast flowers and fruit swags.

Harmoniously horizontal with the low boat bodies, the bold curving forms of the cast handles extend outward in compounded S-curves joined to the rims with shell motifs. In thin bands along the top of the rims, finely engraved diaper panels and scroll borders spread from the handles to the lift of the spouts. Under the rims and spouts engraved diaper panels and scrolls with shell motifs emphasize the delicacy of the rims. These decorative engraved motifs are repeated in variations on the stands.

De Lamerie

7. Stands, 1739

Extreme height: 1⅜ in. (3.5 cm.)
Extreme length: 9⅜ in. (23.8 cm.)
Width: 6¾ in. (17.2 cm.)
Total weight: 38 oz., 17 dwt.
(1,208.375 grams)
1: 19 oz., 6 dwt. (600.644 grams)
2: 19 oz., 11 dwt. (607.731 grams)
m. 77. 2. 3a, b

Hallmarks

De Lamerie's second mark.

Lion passant gardant (Sterling Standard).

Crowned leopard head (London assay).

Lower-case *d* (letter date for 1739).

Struck on center bottoms.

Engraved Arms

Identical to those on sauceboats (cat. no. 6).

Form

In order to be fashionable and functional, large or particularly specialized ("civilized") domestic services of the eighteenth century were expanded with new serving pieces as they were invented. But fashionable pieces were not always functional (e.g., the early double-lipped shape of the sauceboat proved apt to spill or drip), and impractical serving pieces in silver could be melted down and reworked into an improved form. Stands appeared in the 1730s as an alternative to such destruction of sauceboats. These decorative stands evolved from salvers and acted as presenters and drip catchers for the boats in the service of a meal. Soon they became necessary formal adjuncts to the sauceboats in all the most impressive services.

These oval-shaped stands with dished interiors are constructed of two parts: (1) shallow cast rims and (2) a surface worked into up-curving sides with groin-ribbed sections to conform to the alternating patterns of the rim. Four short cast leonine legs applied under the rim support each stand.

The interior engraving reflects the designs engraved around the outer edge of the companion sauceboats. But here the engraving is more fully realized and more heavily chased, giving a strong illusion of relief to the rich scheme of shells, paneled bands, floral clusters, and scrolls. By 1739, when these stands were made, de Lamerie was exploring the close relationship between cast and chased decoration which reached fruition in the 1740s with his rococo style.

8. **Ladles,** ca. 1740

Length: 7⅞ in. (20 cm.)
Width of bowl: 2½ in. (6.4 cm.)
Total weight: 88 oz., 13 dwt.
(2,758.712 grams)
1: 44 oz., 6 dwt. (1,378.470 grams)
2: 44 oz., 7 dwt. (1,380.242 grams)
m. 77. 2. 4a, b

Form

    Ladles were evolved from the basting spoon,
an item, though sometimes made in silver, that
must be considered a kitchen utensil. Soup ladles
first appeared in their current form (round bowls
with curving handles) in the 1720s, when they
were also known as "ragout" spoons (see cat. no.
13). Size and decoration were determined by the
tureen the ladle was intended to serve. So it was
with similar, but smaller, examples that appeared
in the late 1730s as practical afterthoughts, to
accompany the sauceboats that had proliferated
with the increased popularity of sauces in the
English cuisine.

    Easily distinguished as sauce ladles by their size and shape, these ladles have wide, fig-shaped bowls
with curved tapering handles, each ending in an oval cartouche. The flat engraving at the top rim of the
bowls and along the handle repeats that found on both the companion sauceboats and stands. However,
the cartilaginous form of the cartouche and the unusual serpent biting the feathered wing that embel-
lishes it have no source in the designs of the sauceboats and stands. Although these ladles precede de
Lamerie's major rococo works, he was already experimenting with exotic combinations of decorative
motifs.

    The presence on these ladles of only de Lamerie's mark and the lion passant gardant for sterling
would lead to the conclusion that the ladles were ordered at the same time as the stands, since it was
common practice to strike secondary pieces with fewer marks than the major piece. If this is the case, we
can determine that the stands were produced between May of 1739[1] and 27 June 1739, the day that de
Lamerie registered his third mark. The ladles may have been part of this same commission, but they bear
de Lamerie's third mark and thus were not completed until after 27 June.

Hallmarks	Engraved Crest
De Lamerie's third mark.	The crest of Yorke for Phillip Yorke of Erddig, Denbighshire.
Lion passant gardant (Sterling Standard).	
Struck on outer bowl near juncture with handle.	On a wreath, a lion's head erased Proper collared (Gules thereon a bezant).

De Lamerie

9. Kettle on Stand, 1736

Extreme height: 13¼ in. (33.7 cm.)
Extreme width: 9 in. (22.9 cm.)
Kettle height: 9⅞ in. (25.1 cm.)
Kettle diameter: 6½ in. (16.5 cm.)
Stand height: 4 in. (10.2 cm.)
Stand diameter: 4⅞ in. (12.4 cm.)
Total weight: 59 oz., 8 dwt.
(1,848.001 grams)
Kettle: 37 oz., 15 dwt. (1,174.712 grams)
Stand: 21 oz., 13 dwt. (673.289 grams)
m. 75.135.42 a, b

Hallmarks

De Lamerie's second mark.

Lion passant gardant (Sterling Standard).

Crowned leopard head (London assay).

Lower-case *a* (letter date for 1736).

Struck inside applied rim on bottom of kettle and bottom of burner pan. Burner lid struck with maker's mark. Lion passant gardant struck inside top of burner cover.

Engraved Crest and Monogram

Initials *SC* under a baron's coronet (unidentified).

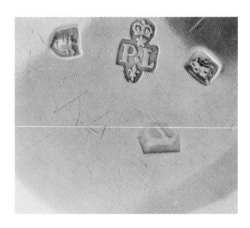

Form

De Lamerie produced several variations on this pumpkin-shaped kettle and three-legged stand throughout the 1730s, decorating them with overall low repoussé relief (see cat. no. 4); with pronounced ribs and engraved embellishment, as seen here; and with applied cast decoration augmented with rich engraving (see cat. no. 10).

This pumpkin-shaped kettle reflects a baroque spirit in its robust vertical ribs and alternating sections. The highly decorative compound curves strengthen the kettle, while hidden hinges make the round lid a smooth continuation of the vessel body. The pine cone finial is reputedly the symbol of hospitality and thus a fitting addition to such a prime serving piece.

The fluted and scrolled S-curve spout, with an extended lower lip that guarantees easy pouring, is one of de Lamerie's most successful. The S-curve is repeated in the refined and embellished sides of the swing handle. Woven wickerwork, now missing, originally provided insulation across the top of the handle. Only in the small grotesque masks inside the upright curves of the handle does de Lamerie indulge himself with a touch of whimsical mannerism in this otherwise controlled composition.

The stand, in a familiar de Lamerie form, is raised on inward curved and scrolled legs ending in lion paw feet; the burner base is attached to these legs by small C-scroll brackets. A pin-and-stop connection located in the close fitting rings of the kettle and stand firmly fastens the two components together, a device preferable to the applied handles of some stands since it allowed the whole unit to be carried securely by the kettle handle.

10. Kettle on Stand with Tray, 1736–37

Extreme height: 14⅝ in. (37.2 cm.)
Extreme width: 9 in. (22.9 cm.)
Kettle height: 10 in. (25.4 cm.)
Kettle diameter: 6⁵/₁₆ in. (16.1 cm.)
Stand height: 4 in. (10.2 cm.)
Stand width: 6 in. (15.2 cm.)
Tray height: 2 in. (5.1 cm.)
Tray diameter: 10⅜ in. (26.4 cm.)
Total weight: 106 oz., 4 dwt.
(3,302.659 grams)
Kettle: 46 oz., 1 dwt. (1,431.625 grams)
Stand: 28 oz., 5 dwt. (878.819 grams)
Tray: 31 oz., 18 dwt. (992.215 grams)
m. 77. 2. 5 a–c

Engraved Arms on Tray

Argent on a fess Azure between three acorns.

Vert three molets Argent.

Impaling Argent three bands Gules on a canton Azure a spur Or (for a Knight of Northamptonshire).

Motto: Seek Liberty.

Arms unidentified.

Hallmarks—Kettle

De Lamerie's second mark.

Lion passant gardant (Sterling Standard).

Crowned leopard head (London assay).

Lower-case *b* (letter date for 1737).

Struck on bottom of kettle.

Scratch engraved 46–6 (for weight).

Hallmarks—Stand

De Lamerie's second mark.

Crowned leopard head (London assay).

Lower-case *a* (letter date for 1736).

Struck on bottom of burner pan.

Scratch engraved 28–9 (for weight).

Hallmarks—Tray

De Lamerie's second mark.

Lion passant gardant (Sterling Standard).

Crowned leopard head (London assay).

Lower-case *b* (letter date for 1737).

Struck on center bottom.

Scratch engraved 32–3 (for weight).

Form

The same basic forms of cat. nos. 4 and 9 are seen here, i.e., the kettle with global or "skittle-ball"-shaped body, S-curved and scrolled spout, swing handle with double-S curves, and the stand with three inward curving scrolled legs to which brackets attach a spirit burner. Beginning with the reign of George I, a kettle commissioned by a wealthy client would have required the additional piece seen here. The tray or salver (used also with sauceboats and other serving pieces) is of practical origins, in this case protecting the table top or cloth from heat, the spirit burner fuel, and the inevitable drips from the kettle's spout. These trays were always "optional extras" and have seldom survived with their kettles.

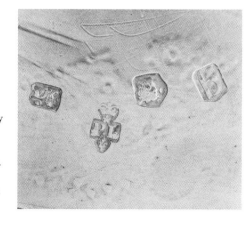

One of de Lamerie's most decorative serving pieces, this kettle on stand with tray illustrates the silversmith's early ability with exuberant yet controlled decoration. The bold decorative castings at first glance appear as independent elements, divided by the smooth polished surfaces. Cast shell and scroll forms applied at the swing handle hinge and below the knob establish an irregular silhouette and focus attention near the top of the kettle. The bold applied cast relief of the escutcheon on each side of the body reinforces this focus with the upturned head of the demi-cherub who clutches the escutcheon as if in support.

De Lamerie provides a transition from relief forms to smooth surface with extremely fine engraving. At the shoulder this takes the form of shell, scroll, and panel motifs, which are also repeated on the tray. Framing the decorative relief surrounding the escutcheon are extensions of the cast leaf and twig forms as well as soft cloud patterns.

11. Punch Ladle, 1738

Length: 14 5/16 in. (37.2 cm.)
Width of bowl: 3½ in. (8.9 cm.)
Total weight: 13 oz., 7 dwt.
(414.604 grams)
m. 77. 2.6

Hallmarks

De Lamerie's second mark.

Lion passant gardant (Sterling Standard).

Crowned leopard head (struck twice)
(London assay).

Lower-case *c* (letter date for 1738).

Struck on underside of bowl near rim.

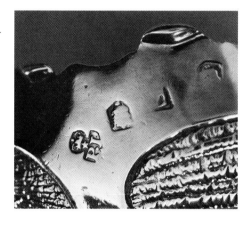

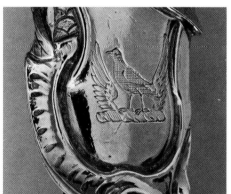

Form

The punch ladle appeared in the last decade of the seventeenth century with the creation of the silver monteith or punch bowl. Appearing first as a small shallow cup with ring handle, resembling a French wine taster, the punch ladle soon developed a long turned wood or tubular silver handle for greater ease of use. The long, straight handle is joined to the circular or oval bowl at a 45-degree angle, which permits the bowl to be plunged to the bottom of the punch bowl and retrieved while always remaining horizontal. By 1740 punch ladle bowls were being produced in a variety of shapes. Later, in the second half of the eighteenth century, these bowls became smaller as the custom for drinking shifted from quantities of weak punch to smaller amounts of more highly intoxicating beverages.

Engraved Crest

On a wreath, in a vol displayed (Argent or Proper) a bird Sable.

Unidentified.

De Lamerie

The scalloped rim of this cast oval bowl is entwined with vine and ivy leaves in low relief. The bottom of the bowl is cast to resemble a ribbed shell, partially cradled in strapwork. The handle's straight cast shaft is crossed by panels and strapwork, while the whole is twined with ivy leaves and berries. Scale panels and shell forms frame the engraved crest just below the shell volute.

Phillips suggests that this ladle is unique in de Lamerie's works.[1] Although the complex decoration and the maker's mark identify this piece as his creation, it is nevertheless possible, judging from the minimal chasing of the cast surfaces, that it is not a product of his own hands. Close inspection of the handle shows the stiffness of the low-relief decoration, which is also uncharacteristic of de Lamerie. Phillips notwithstanding, no evidence exists to prove that de Lamerie ever made spoons,[2] which were traditionally the products of spoon makers. It is therefore likely that this ladle is an example of a design by de Lamerie executed at another shop specializing in spoons. The ladle would have been struck with de Lamerie's mark before its sale to indicate that it was de Lamerie who had received the commission.[3] Should this be the case, the punch ladle is still unique and an equally rare example of de Lamerie's ornamental design executed by another hand.

1. Phillips, p. 103.
2. Miss Susan Hare, Librarian, The Worshipful Company of Goldsmiths, London.
3. This was a common practice with silversmiths receiving large commissions that included items they did not normally produce.

12. Pair of Covered Soup Tureens, 1722–42

(With liners by Wakelin and Garrard, Ltd., 1795)

Tureens

Extreme height: 11 in. (28 cm.)
Extreme width: 15⅛ in. (38.4 cm.)
Diameter: 11⅛ in. (28.3 cm.)
Total weight: 310 oz., 11 dwt.
(9,660.922 grams)
1: 155 oz., 17 dwt. (4,847.679 grams)
2: 154 oz., 14 dwt. (4,812.243 grams)
m. 77.2.7 a–f

Liners

Depth: 4⁵/₁₆ in. (11.3 cm.)
Diameter: 10¹³/₁₆ in. (27.5 cm.)
Total weight: 54 oz., 9 dwt.
(1,793.453 grams)
1: 26 oz., 18 dwt. (835.896 grams)
2: 27 oz., 11 dwt. (857.557 grams)

Hallmarks—Tureens

De Lamerie's first mark.

Britannia (Britannia Standard).

Capital *G* (letter date for 1722).

Struck on center bottoms of bowls.

Hallmarks—Liners

John Wakelin's and Robert Garrard I's first mark as partners.

Lion passant gardant (Sterling Standard).

Lower-case *u* (letter date for 1795).

Monarch's head (George III) (duty stamp).

Two indistinct marks.

Struck on center bottom.

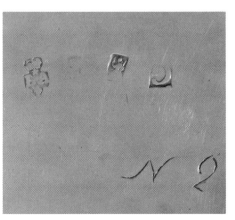

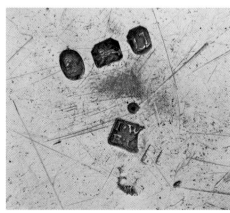

continued

Engraved Arms on Lids

Edgcumbe for Richard Edgcumbe, created Baron Mount Edgcumbe, 20 April 1742, died 1758.

Gules on bend Sable cotised Or three boar's heads couped Argent.

Supporters: two greyhounds Argent gutty Sable about the necks collars dovetailed Gules.

Motto: *Au plaisir fort de Dieu* ("At the all-powerful disposal of God").[1]

Engraved Crest on Bowls and Liners

On a wreath, a boar passant Argent about the neck a wreath of oak Proper.

A baron's coronet above.

Form

The earliest silver soup tureens emulated the forms in Chinese and Meissen porcelain that had popularized this serving dish in the early eighteenth century.[2] These first tureens in silver had oval bowls standing on a flaring oval foot and were covered with a high conical domed lid, rising to a baluster finial or ring handle. With the change of the tureen bowls to a round shape, the central foot was replaced with four small scrolled feet. These feet and fixed up-curving or ring handles at the ends of the bowl appeared in the mid-1720s. Low domed lids replaced the high conical ones early in the 1720s.

From the date stamped on this pair of tureens, they appear to be the earliest known tureens by de Lamerie and are possibly the earliest extant silver tureens made in England. They have survived, however, not in their original form, but in a mixed style indicating that they were altered at a later date. The earliest element is the low, domed covers with applied cast decorations: little has been changed on these covers but the handles. The present inverted U-shaped handles replaced earlier oval ring handles which can still be seen on other tureens from the 1720s. The present handles straddle a raised area with a plain, polished surface that served as juncture for the previous handles. The central flat-button form in this area covers the opening made for the original joint between handle and cover.

The pleasant swelling bowls of these tureens recall the tureens ordered in London by Empress Catherine the Great and made in about 1726 by Simon Pantin[3] (now in the Hermitage Museum, Leningrad). The bowls and covers of the Pantin tureens are decorated with applied forms similar to, though less sophisticated than, those on the Gilbert tureen covers. Close inspection of the Gilbert tureen bowls supports the idea that they originally resembled the Pantin bowls. Their round shape now offers no evidence of the rich engraving that can be seen on de Lamerie's tureens in Woburn Abbey, which date from 1723 and were heretofore considered his oldest extant tureens.[4]

The walls of the Gilbert bowls are thick and even. The survival of the original hallmarks reinforces the conclusion that the bowls themselves were changed little through reworking; perhaps only applied decorations similar to those on the covers and feet were removed and the bowl surfaces repolished.

The applied cast decoration, legs, and handles of the Gilbert tureens are similar to those of a tureen by de Lamerie dated 1738.[5] This tureen gives several clues to the possible dating of the redecorating of the pair seen here. The fixed U-shaped handles on the bowls and covers resemble in shape and concept those of the 1738 tureen. The cast scrolled frames applied to the sides of the tureens are all from the same molds, with identical leafy twig, wheat sheaf, and corn cob embellishments. These identical castings are particularly important aids in dating the reworked tureens since de Lamerie never used the same molds for long. On the 1738 tureens, massive applied frontal lion masks decorate the joint with the leonine legs, each entwined with a tail, that terminate with claws clutching spheres. De Lamerie had used this leg form as early as 1732. The Gilbert tureens are raised on an elaborate, and therefore later, variation of this leg. The up-stretched demi-lions that balance one another demonstrate de Lamerie's transition from the earlier idea to the undulating, elaborately conceived and executed high relief of his rococo period.

From such a stylistic analysis, it is probable that the reworking occurred about 1739 or 1740, but certainly before 1742. Close inspection of the engraved escutcheons now bearing the crest of Baron Mount Edgcumbe reveals that they previously bore more elaborate engraving (full arms), which was replaced by the Mount Edgcumbe crest. Since the Edgcumbe family held no claim to arms before 1742, it could only mean that a previous titled owner had, in fact, commissioned the reworking and then sold the pair of tureens to the Edgcumbes sometime after 1740.

Liners, 1795

Plain hemispheric sterling liners, commissioned by the second Baron Mount Edgcumbe, were created to fit within these de Lamerie tureens. These liners are eighteenth-century improvements on the tureen, permitting easier cleaning of the food-containing element and utilization of the outer shell of the tureen as a hot water jacket for greater heat retention in the food. Small cast shell handles on the rims of the liners are provided for ease of removal from the enclosing tureens. On the inside bottom of the liners are engraved the crest of Mount Edgcumbe surmounted with an earl's coronet.

1. H. P. Jones, p. 193.
2. Charles Kandler produced a silver tureen marked for the year 1729 in the same form used by the first European porcelain factory at Meissen till about 1740.
3. Hayward, pl. 65A.
4. Clayton, p. 267, pl. 43.
5. Phillips, p. 102, pl. CXX.

13. Pair of Soup Ladles, 1748

Length: 13¾ in. (34.9 cm.)
Width of bowls: 3¹³/₁₆ in. (9.7 cm.)
Total weight: 23 oz., 4 dwt.
(721.127 grams)
1: 11 oz., 9 dwt. (356.134 grams)
2: 11 oz., 15 dwt. (364.993 grams)
m. 77.2.8a,b

Hallmarks

De Lamerie's third mark.

Lion passant gardant (Sterling Standard).

Crowned leopard head (London assay).

Lower-case *n* (letter date for 1748).

Struck on outside bottom of bowls.

Engraved Crest

Crest of Mount Edgcumbe for Richard Edgcumbe, created Baron Mount Edgcumbe, 20 April 1742, died 1758.

On a wreath, a boar Argent, about the neck a wreath of oak Proper (variant for that recorded as boar passant).

A baron's coronet above.

Form

The basic form of soup ladles changed little from their inception in about 1720. Produced en suite with tureens and sauceboats, they reflect in the treatments of the handles the decorative schemes of the containers they serve.

From the engraving style and worn appearance of the Mount Edgcumbe crests on the handles of this pair of ladles, it is safe to conclude that the engraving is contemporary with their manufacture. They were therefore commissioned by the first Baron Mount Edgcumbe, unlike the tureens they serve, which were altered at least five, and possibly seven, years earlier.

The cast scrolls decorating the ladle handles are in de Lamerie's rococo style of the late 1740s[1] and not related to the earlier decorative scheme of the tureens, another indication that the ladles were an isolated commission, independent from the tureens themselves.

These ladles are the latest works in the Gilbert Collection bearing the maker's mark of Paul de Lamerie.

1.   See cat. no. 11 and its note 2.

14. Pair of Candlesticks, 1741

Height: 8¼ in. (21 cm.)
Width of base: 5⁹/₁₆ in. (14.2 cm.)
Total weight: 44 oz., 10 dwt.
(1,385.567 grams)
1: 23 oz., 9 dwt. (729.987 grams)
2: 21 oz., 1 dwt. (655.570 grams)
m. 77.1.11a,b

Hallmarks

De Lamerie's third mark.

Lion passant gardant (Sterling Standard).

Crowned leopard head (London assay).

Lower-case *f* (letter date for 1741).

Struck inside cast bases.

Scratch engraved: 1—no. 3; 2—no. 1.

Engraved Crests

Out of a mural crown two arms flexed, vested, and holding a shield.

Possibly the crest of Ridge of Tyning House, Sussex.[1]

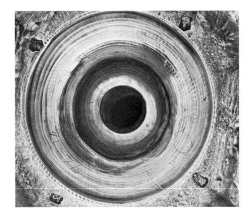

Form

Candlesticks provided easily portable lighting devices for table and chamber use. Sets of two, four, and occasionally six were made to augment the primary lighting (chandeliers and/or candelabra) and to provide light for a specific activity (for example, gaming tables incorporated platforms at each corner to accommodate candlesticks).

Early eighteenth-century candlesticks occur in a variety of baluster forms. These forms, repeated in innumerable variations, increased in size and density of decoration until supplanted by other forms at mid-century. Short candlesticks (to four inches) are called desk candlesticks. Small candlesticks (to about six inches) are generally intended for use in toilet services. Larger sticks (about seven inches and taller) are identified for table use in inventories of the period.

The baluster form of these Gilbert candlesticks debuted about 1720[2] and is identifiable by its cast, nearly square base with concave corners and by the distinctive ring at the foot of the high-hipped baluster stem. This form was used by other silversmiths besides de Lamerie, and retained its popularity into the 1750s.

Since detachable nozzles (or wax pans) to protect highly decorated candlesticks from hot wax were not invented until the 1740s, these examples were probably created without them.

1. Both Fairbairn's *Book of Crests* and Burke's *General Armory* list this crest without tinctures, which suggests that the crest had originated separately from the family arms and had been assumed without a grant from the King of Arms.
2. Clayton, p. 37.
3. Phillips, pl. CXII, 1735; pl. CXL, 1737; and pl. CXXXII, 1741.

De Lamerie created three variations of the baluster candlestick, in 1735, 1737, and 1741.[3] The earliest version is composed of plain surfaces, with ogival molded base, square baluster stem, and plain banded socket. The versions for 1737 and 1741 are most similar, sharing common decorative parts. Surprisingly, the 1737 pair of candlesticks is more elaborate than that in the Gilbert Collection, although the elaboration occurs only in some parts, such as the sockets, while others, such as the bases, are far simpler. De Lamerie worked to perfect his designs, and in the variations among his three pairs of candlesticks we see the process of trial, error, and correction. In the Gilbert candlesticks he has balanced the elements to produce a composition of particularly pleasing integrity of form and rhythmic decoration. Shell motifs unite the whole, recurring at the sockets, at the hip of the baluster stem, at the moundlike juncture of stem and base, and at the corners and sides of the nearly square base.

15. Basket, 1741

Extreme height: 10¼ in. (26 cm.)
Extreme width: 12³/₁₆ in. (31 cm.)
Basket height: 4 in. (10.2 cm.)
Basket length: 14⁷/₁₆ in. (38 cm.)
Total weight: 55 oz., 3 dwt.
(1,715.115 grams)
m. 77.1.3

Form

In the five years following the introduction of the single swing handle basket in about 1735, the structure of this useful container changed in small but significant ways. The plain cast or twisted ring, once positioned at the inner shoulder of the basket, was replaced with a heavier cast sculptural ring applied to the fragile outer rim of the basket. This cast rim protects the most vulnerable edge of the thin metal and provides a solid structural element on which to anchor the hinge of the handle. At the same time, the pierced foot ring changed to a solid cast band raised on four scrolled feet that form an integral part of the decoration. Cast elements made this new form of basket heavier and therefore more expensive to produce than previous baskets. As though it had to be made more visually impressive to account for the added manufacturing costs, after 1740 the basket became an increasingly decorative rococo creation.

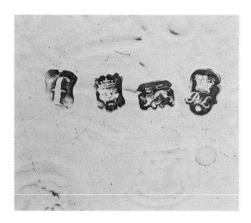

Hallmarks

De Lamerie's third mark.

Lion passant gardant (Sterling Standard).

Crowned leopard head (London assay).

Lower-case *f* (letter date for 1741).

Struck under basket bottom, near foot ring.

Engraved Arms

The arms, coronet, and supporters of Marsham with Pym in pretense.

Argent a lion passant Gules between two bendlets Azure, a scocheon in pretense Sable a bull's head couped Argent in a wreath Or and Azure.

The shield ensigned with a baron's coronet.

Supporters: two lions crusily collared with a mural crown.

Motto: *Non sibi sed patriae* ("Not for oneself, but for one's country").

De Lamerie

This basket produced early in de Lamerie's rococo decade (the 1740s), though of very restrained oval form, is a light, airy creation of scrolls and shells. The sides are decorated with contrasting panels of large- and small-scale X-shaped piercing, bordered by patterns of pierced scrolls and shells. The base ring is cast with four scrolled feet, each with a draped cherub mask, that alternate with shells at the sides and ends. On the shaped and cast top rim, large applied shells extend from the ends. Leaf forms reinforce the juncture of the rim with the handle hinge and embellish the simple handle. In subsequent baskets, de Lamerie used freer decorative motifs and more elaborate castings but retained the same structural form.

16. Pair of Salvers, 1741

Height: 2⅞ in. (7.3 cm.)
Diameter: 18½ in. (47 cm.)
Total weight: 205 oz., 10 dwt.
(6,392.7 grams)
1: 105 oz., 5 dwt. (3,274.310 grams)
2: 100 oz., 5 dwt. (3,118.390 grams)
m. 77.1.6a,b

Hallmarks

De Lamerie's third mark.

Lion passant gardant (Sterling Standard).

Crowned leopard head (London assay).

1: Lower-case *f* (letter date for 1741).

2: Lower-case *g* (letter date for 1742).

Struck on bottom near edge.

Engraved Arms

The arms of Coote impaling Newport, an earl's coronet above, the combined supporters of the Earls of Montrath and Bradford. For Charles Henry Coote, Earl of Montrath (Irish title), who married Diana Newport, daughter of Richard, Earl of Bradford, 1721.[1]

Argent a chevron between three coots Sable (Coote).

Impaling Argent a chevron between three leopard faces Sable (hatched as Gules) (Newport).

The shield ensigned with an earl's coronet.

Supporters: a wolf with a crown about the neck and a leopard gardant.

Motto: *Vincit veritas* ("Truth conquers").

Form

Although only rare examples survive from before the Restoration, the small circular tray called a salver dates from the Middle Ages, when it was used to carry a low cup of food to be sampled by a taster—a common precaution in a time when poisoning was widespread. The word *salver* may thus have been derived from the Spanish *salvar,* meaning "to preserve."[2]

This serving piece, separate from its cup, continued throughout the seventeenth century in a circular, crimped-edge shape raised on a central trumpet-shaped foot. In the early eighteenth century various new shapes appeared, such as trefoils, quatrefoils, octafoils, squares, etc., but the circular form continued to predominate. By 1715 the central foot had been replaced by three or more cast feet attached to the applied cast rim, which became a distinguishing feature of eighteenth-century salvers.

1. These arms are engraved as though Diana Newport was the heiress to her father's title, for upon marriage with a peer's heiress the husband is entitled to the sinister (left) supporter of his wife's paternal coat of arms (Porney, *Elements of Heraldry,* London, 1975, p. 239). No evidence of this descendant exists.
2. Clayton, p. 236.
3. Ibid., ill. 468.

The composition of these circular salvers offers a spectacular example of why de Lamerie was considered a leading manufacturer of both decorative and serviceable plate. The flat surfaces of the salvers are visually extended and protected by the cast sculptural rims applied to them. These undulating rococo confections combine vine, leaf, and grape clusters with masks in shell and scroll frames. Even the cast scrollwork with lion masks and paws that forms the four legs is a visual continuation of the sculptural rims. Of particular importance to the composition is the fine engraving of the flat surface, which forms a wide band that spreads inward from the rims, providing a transition from the crusty sculpture at the edge to the plain polished surface surrounding the arms. In 1745 de Lamerie created a second pair of salvers for the same patron, the Earl of Montrath, but they are far more regular and less dynamically rococo in composition and execution.[3]

17. Ewer and Basin, 1742

Ewer
Extreme height: 18¼ in. (46.5 cm.)
Extreme width: 13¾ in. (35 cm.)
Diameter of base: 7 in. (17.8 cm.)
Basin
Diameter: 29 in. (73.7 cm.)
Total weight: 541 oz., 12 dwt.
(13,745.090 grams)
Ewer: 125 oz., 2 dwt. (3,890.900 grams)
Basin: 316 oz., 10 dwt. (9,844.190 grams)
m. 77.2.9a,b

Hallmarks

De Lamerie's third mark.

Lion passant gardant (Sterling Standard).

Crowned leopard head (London assay).

Lower-case *g* (letter date for 1742).

Struck on underside of basin and on the plain
panel near handle (at back of figure).

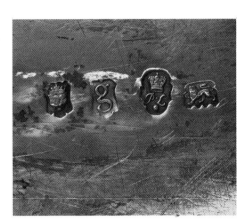

Cast Arms on Ewer

Arms of Coote impaling Newport, an earl's
coronet above, the combined supporters of the
Earls of Montrath and Bradford. For Charles
Henry Coote, Earl of Montrath (Irish title), who
married Diana Newport, daughter of Richard,
Earl of Bradford, 1721 (see cat. no. 16).

Argent a chevron between three coots Sable (Coote).

Impaling Argent a chevron between three leopard
faces Sable (Newport).

The shield ensigned with an earl's coronet.

Supporters: a wolf with a crown about the neck
and a leopard gardant.

Motto: *Vincit veritas* ("Truth conquers").

Patch marks indicate that cast arms were also originally applied (by bolting) to the center of the
basin. These arms do not survive.

Form

The ewer and basin were important elements of domestic plate from medieval times on. At intervals during a meal they were circulated so that guests could wash the accumulated food from their fingers with scented water before being served the next course. With the acceptance of the fork in the late seventeenth century, the ewer and basin (or dish) passed from table use. The forms survived as purely decorative sideboard ornaments, and their importance as such is evidenced by the numerous examples included in corporation plate, guildhall plate, and domestic plate of large country houses.

continued

Gremio: *". . . my house within the city is richly fur-*
nished with plate and gold, Basons and ewers
to lave her dainty hands:. . ."[1]

The apex of eighteenth-century decorative corporate plate must be de Lamerie's ewer and dish for The Worshipful Company of Goldsmiths, of 1741.[2] No commission could have been more important or more gratifying to the silversmith than to be chosen over his peers to produce the focal point of his livery company's sideboard plate. To de Lamerie, it was tantamount to being first warden (an office he never achieved).

The concept for the ewer and basin he devised for that commission was in keeping with the Huguenot revival (ca. 1700) of the helmet-shaped ewer and wide-rimmed shallow basin. The decorative scheme with which de Lamerie embellished that set is the prototype for the Gilbert ewer and basin. The year the Goldsmiths' commission was completed brought the order from Algernon, the sixth Earl of Montrath, for another ewer and basin. (Even though the earl's rank or social position did not merit a ewer and basin rivaling that of the Goldsmiths' Company, his wealth did.) This commission provided the opportunity for de Lamerie to resolve the problems of his earlier design scheme. His second chance shows how he reworked and improved that most important commission.

The broad border of the Gilbert dish is divided into eight distinct scrolled panels, with alternating scenic and shell patterns. At the top,[3] Jupiter appears with his attributes—an eagle and lightning bolts—while Amphitrite, the wife of Poseidon, is depicted at the bottom in her dolphin-drawn sea chariot, being returned to Poseidon for their nuptials. (This female figure is probably based on a seventeenth-century Dutch engraving.)[4] At either side are amorini with heads turned toward the center. To the left the figure holds up a large shell of pearls; to the right the figure holds on his shoulder a cornucopia overflowing with coins—allegories representing the riches of the sea and land.

Among the high reliefs of the border are myriad small earth and sea creatures, flowers, and shells. Curiously, among the shells embellishing the strapwork scrolls that partition the border into eight panels are residual auricular forms, like echoes of the mannerism of the de Lamerie kettle on stand (cat. no. 4).

Supporting the helmet-shaped ewer is a kneeling, bat-winged amorino on a rounded base richly chased with waves and a dolphin's head. Dominating the surface of the ewer proper is the applied figure of Poseidon rising from the waves. To the left and right of the wide spout are cherubic representations of the winds. The whole body of the ewer is divided into panels with scrolled shaped work similar to that on the accompanying basin.

The focal point of the ewer is the large female demi-figure that serves as handle, counterbalancing the ewer's lip. This handle, compared with that of the Goldsmiths' Company ewer, presents a more complete composition, a fuller resolution by de Lamerie of problems in the earlier design. The Goldsmiths' ewer has a handle with a male figure that also turns back toward the lip, but the handle is visually pulled from the ewer, lacking the compositional unity of de Lamerie's ewer of the next year.

1. *The Taming of the Shrew*, act 2, scene 1. William Shake-speare, *Comedies, Histories and Tragedies*, facsimile edi-tion, New Haven, 1954, p. 217.
2. Ordered in 1740 as partial replacement for silver melted down as a donation by the Goldsmiths' Company to the rebuilding of London after the fire of 1666.
3. Sideboard plate basins were displayed standing on edge.
4. A scene from the same print of Perseus rescuing An-dromeda can be seen adorning the center of an oval silver-gilt dish created in Augsbury, ca. 1650. See Chris-tie's *Bicentennial Review*, 1966, p. 148.

18. Two-Handled Covered Cup, 1742

Silver gilt
Extreme height: 15¾ in. (39.9 cm.)
Extreme width: 9⅝ in. (24.5 cm.)
Diameter of lip: 6¼ in. (15.9 cm.)
Diameter of base: 5 in. (12.7 cm.)
Total weight: 102 oz., 11 dwt.
(3,189.262 grams)
m. 77.2.10a,b

Hallmarks

De Lamerie's third mark.

Lion passant gardant (Sterling Standard).

Crowned leopard head (London assay).

Lower-case *g* (letter date for 1742).

Struck inside lid and inside stem on base of cup.

Form

The form of the two-handled covered cup changed little between 1717 and 1730, but in the hands of de Lamerie during the thirties and forties, it became a piece of decorative sculpture. Exploring surface decoration more than form, he produced a series of cups in those years that illustrates the evolution of his rococo style.

In the early 1730s, de Lamerie broke with his inherently French style and began to invent more elaborate and imaginative decorative schemes. In 1732 he produced a two-handled cup[1] with bold caryatid and Atlas figures encircling the handles. Although these forms of applied decoration were new, they were still clustered in traditional areas: the cover, handles, lower cup, and base. This composition and the wide band of plain polished surface below the lip mark the cup as an early effort.

In 1739 de Lamerie abandoned his earlier cup shapes. Two examples of covered cups from this year[2] show a more vertical format, with the cup body echoing the conical dome of the covers. It is this form that de Lamerie used three years later in creating the complex decorative scheme and cohesive overall design of the covered cup seen here.

The entire surface of this cup is organized into panels by strapwork, scrolls, and volutes. Natural forms—ivy, grapevines, flowers, and shells—predominate, each symbolizing some aspect of the Bacchus myth. Ivy was sacred to Bacchus because a thick shoot of it suddenly grew up to screen him from the celestial fire of his father, Zeus, which consumed his mother, Semele, before his birth. Shells are associated with Bacchus in another version of his birth, in which Semele was punished for her liaison with Zeus by being shut into a chest that was thrown into the sea. The chest, carried by the waves to Peloponnesus, was opened to reveal the mother dead and the child alive.[3]

The infant Bacchus is depicted in the central panels on each side of this cup. On one side he kneels in a vineyard, making wine in a vat. On the other he sits in a forest glade, holding clusters of grapes and a musical instrument, symbols of the revels associated with his worship.

The general nature of its decorations made this cup one that could be presented on many occasions, and de Lamerie apparently repeated the design several times. Such silver items could be produced from the same molds in considerable numbers, and only the chased or carved details would reflect the silversmith's own variations. A comparison between the Gilbert cup and a nearly identical one, also of 1742, in the Sterling and Francis Clark Art Institute,[4] gives a clue to the dating of these cups. On the Clark cup, the infant Bacchus is seated on the roots of a sloping tree trunk. On the Gilbert cup, the chased tree trunk rises more directly, apart from the figure, providing a strong vertical element. To the right of the figure on the Clark cup is a diagonal line of rustic fencing that continues the line of the infant's leg, body, and arm toward the upper right. On the Gilbert cup, no such fence appears in the background; only leaf forms parallel the diagonals of the figure. Since de Lamerie's evolution in style was away from the verticals and horizontals of formal French-style cups toward a more dynamic rococo exuberance, it would be logical to assume that the Gilbert cup, with its more rigid chasing, was the first of these two cups to be produced in 1742.

1. Clayton, p. 100 and pl. 210.
2. Grimwade, 1974, pl. 6 and pl. 8, attributed to de Lamerie.
3. *Larousse Encyclopedia of Mythology*, pp. 178–79.
4. *Art News*, LII, p. 28, and Phillips, p. 107, ill. CXXXVIII, dated 1742.

De Lamerie

Nicholas Sprimont English, 1716–1771 19. **Basket**, ca. 1745

Extreme height: 11½ in. (29.2 cm.)
Extreme length: 18 in. (45.7 cm.)
Extreme width: 13½ in. (34.2 cm.)
Basket height: 5¼ in. (13 cm.)
Base length: 10¼ in. (26 cm.)
Base width: 8 in. (20.3 cm.)
Total weight: 91 oz., 3 dwt.
(2,834.900 grams)
m. 77.1.10

Born in Liège, Belgium—23 January 1716
Apprenticed to his uncle, Nicholas Joseph
    Sprimont, in Liège—1730
Arrived in England and entered only mark (Ster-
    ling Standard), Compton Street, Soho—1742
Apparently made little, if any, silver after 1746
Became Manager of the Chelsea porcelain
    factory—1749–58, during the Raised Anchor
    (1749–52) and Red Anchor (1752–56) periods
Became proprietor of the Chelsea factory during the
    Gold Anchor period (1756–69)—1758–69
Retired from factory due to ill health—1769
Died—1771

Engraved Cipher

AFW—unidentified.

From the style of the engraving and the wear evident on the frames surrounding these ciphers, it is
evident that the original arms were removed and
the ciphers added much later, near the end of the
Victorian era.

Hallmarks

Nicholas Sprimont's second mark.

Struck under rim between head and handle.

Like many other pieces made to "special order"
during the eighteenth century, this basket has no
hallmarks beyond the maker's mark; the law required only that items "set for sale" be assayed.
Royal commissions and items to be exported were
also exempt from marks, as were the innumerable
items made of assayed silver melted down from
earlier pieces.

Form

See cat. no. 15.
    The cast elements on this basket illustrate
the effect of the rococo taste on the earlier pierced
basket form.

Very few of Sprimont's silver pieces have survived. This basket is a large, late example in his robust
rococo style of the mid-1740s. In the cast female heads at either end of this basket, one can see Sprimont's
delicate interpretation of the human form.[1] This same sculptural sense is evident in the numerous
figurative pieces produced in soft paste porcelain at the Chelsea Porcelain Factory under his management
and subsequent ownership.[2] His interest in both silver and porcelain was seminal in creating many early
serviceable items in porcelain patterned after silver prototypes.
    In this silver basket, based on a well-known form, Sprimont's own contributions can be seen in the
following elements: the cast base ring and open shell-like feet; the sweet features of the large female heads;
and the subtle casting of the swing handle. This handle, rising in two shafts of wheat stalks, curves
gently at the tassels and then springs upward again to form an arched handle of interlaced bands and
starflowers. These motifs restate in curvilinear form the pattern of the pierced sides and cast rim.

1. Hillier, p. 118.
2. Richard Ormond, "Silver Shapes in Chelsea Porcelain,"
   Country Life, 1 February 1968.

James Bland   Elizabeth Bland

English, dates unknown

James Bland

Apprenticed to his father, Cornelius Bland, a
   silversmith, at Jewin Street, London—
   1 November 1786
Apprenticeship transferred to Thomas Young,
   silversmith, Aldergate Street, London—
   7 February 1787
Freedom unrecorded
Only mark entered (Sterling Standard), in partnership with Elizabeth Bland (believed widow of
   Cornelius Bland), 126 Bunhill Row,
   London—16 September 1794

Elizabeth Bland

Only mark recorded as above—16 September 1794

20.   **Wine Cistern**, 1794

Height: 26 in. (66 cm.)
Length: 35 in. (88.9 cm.)
Width: 24 in. (61 cm.)
Total weight: 1,146 oz., 17 dwt.
(35,670.787 grams)
m. 77.2.11

Hallmarks

James and Elizabeth Bland's first mark.

Lion passant gardant (Sterling Standard).

Crowned leopard head (London assay).

Lower-case *t* (letter date for 1794).

Monarch's head (George III) (duty stamp).

Struck outside on bottom of basin.

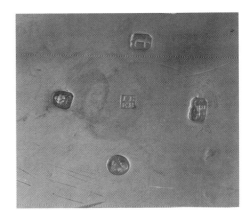

continued

Applied Arms

Arms, as borne after 1801,[1] of Augustus Frederick, Duke of Sussex; with the Garter, coronet, supporters, and motto.

Quarterly 1 & 4, Gules three leopards Or (England).

2, Or a lion in a double tressure counterflory Gules (Scotland).

3, Azure a harp Or stringed Argent (Ireland) in pretense a scocheon tierced in pairle reversed (a) Gules two leopards Or, (b) Or semy of hearts Gules a lion rampant Azure, (c) Gules a horse galloping Argent (Hanover).

Over-all label (omitted here: Argent charged with two hearts and a cross Gules).

The Garter, about the shield.

About the coronet of a royal duke.

Supporters: a leopard Or royally crowned Proper and a unicorn Argent about the neck of the coronet of a royal duke Or, both charged on the shoulder with a label as in the arms.

Motto: *Deus pro nobis qui contra nos* ("With God in our favor, who can avail against us?").

These arms were probably applied at both sides of the cistern originally, but now on the reverse side are those added about 1843, as follows:

Arms of Lt. Col. George Hussey (1796–1874) of Prestwold Hall, who married in 1824 Mary Anne Lydia, daughter of John Heathcote, of Conington Castle, Hunts.

Quarterly 1 & 4, Quarterly Sable and Or.

1, a cinquefoil Ermine (Packe).

2, Or a cross Vert.

3, barry Ermine and Gules; impaling Ermine three roundels Gules each charged with a crest Or (Heathcote).

Motto: *Libertas sub rege pio* ("Liberty under a pious king").

The whole upon a mantle.

On a wreath, a lion's head erased Or collared Sable thereon three cinquefoils Ermine.

On a wreath, in front of a tree a doe looking backwards.

From the style of casting and engraving, it is likely that these arms were applied about 1843, when acquired by George Hussey at the sale of the Duke of Sussex silver.

Augustus Frederick (sixth son of George III), Duke of Sussex, is remembered as a mild man and a "modest patron of the Arts."[4] That such a monumental wine cistern was commissioned by (or even for) a modest man tells much about the taste of the times. Near the end of the eighteenth century, silver cisterns grew in size and sometimes in height. This example, certainly one of the tallest ever created in England, was intended to stand on the floor, alone or perhaps below a tall sideboard. When filled with ice or ice water its capacity is well over a dozen bottles, indicating the scale on which the royal family entertained. Though essentially refined, the chased, repoussé, and cast neoclassical decorations around the deep basin (acanthus leaves, bellflowers, grape swags, and lion heads) are exaggerated to almost unrecognizable proportions. The long, splayed legs are unusually placed on this cistern: previously four-legged cisterns had legs paired near the ends of the basin, but here the legs quarter the oval basin. Bold acanthus leaves provide a transition from the lion paw and leg feet to the leaf-chased bottom of the basin. The extraordinary size of this piece make its survival most unusual. Such exuberant and massive creations have seldom survived the inevitable changes of taste and periodic financial reversals that have traditionally decimated domestic silver.

Form

Wine cisterns (containers for cooling bottles of wine during banquets) are known to have been used from the Middle Ages to about 1873.[2] Adapted from the large tubs of wood, copper, ceramic, or brass used during the Renaissance, the silver wine cistern appeared in the mid-seventeenth century as a large shallow oval basin raised on four feet. By the beginning of the eighteenth century a single flaring foot had replaced the less stable four feet, providing a more secure base for the heavy cistern. With the altered foot the basin became deeper and, as indicated in eighteenth-century inventories,[3] the cistern was used on side tables for rinsing wine glasses between courses. Their size (exceeded only by silver furniture and a very few chandeliers) obviously made these useful basins a prime status symbol as well.

1. The arms were assigned to Augustus Frederick by his father in 1789. In 1801 the quarter previously included for France was discontinued.
2. When they were replaced by individual wine coolers (see cat. no. 27).
3. Cisterns are alternately referred to there as "baths."
4. Priestley, p. 18.

Paul Storr   English, 1771–1844

Silver gilt
Height: 5¼ in. (13.3 cm.)
Length: 20½ in. (52.1 cm.)
Width: 16 in. (40.6 cm.)
Total weight: 275 oz., 14 dwt.
(8,575.573 grams)
m. 77.1.4

Apprenticed to Andrew Fogelberg, 30 Church
    Street, Soho, London—1785
Freed from apprenticeship—1792
First mark entered (Sterling Standard), with
    William Frisbee as partner, 5 Cock Lane, Snow
    Hill, London—2 May 1792
Second mark entered (Sterling Standard), alone,
    30 Church Street, Soho, London—12 January
    1793
Third mark entered (Sterling Standard), same
    address—27 April 1793
Fourth mark entered (Sterling Standard), same
    address—8 August 1794
Moved to 8 Air Street, Piccadilly, London—
    8 October 1796
Fifth mark entered (Sterling Standard), same
    address—29 November 1799
Sixth mark entered (Sterling Standard), 53 Dean
    Street, Soho, London, under the name of Storr
    and Co., working with Rundell & Bridge—
    21 August 1807
Seventh mark entered (Sterling Standard), same
    address—18 February 1808
Eighth mark entered (Sterling Standard, for
    jewelry), same address—15 December 1808
Storr made partner in Rundell, Bridge & Rundell,
    date unknown[1]—ca. 1811
Ninth mark entered (Sterling Standard, three
    sizes), same address—21 October 1813
Tenth mark entered (Sterling Standard, three
    sizes), same address—12 September 1817
Partnership ending with Rundell, Bridge & Run-
    dell, moved to 17 Harrison Street, Grays Inn
    Road, London—4 March 1819
Eleventh mark entered (Sterling Standard, three
    sizes), same address—2 September 1833
Twelfth (last) mark entered (Sterling Standard),
    same address—17 December 1834

Hallmarks

Storr's third mark.

Lion passant gardant (Sterling Standard).

Crowned leopard head (London assay).

Capital *B* (letter date for 1797).

Monarch's head (George III) (duty stamp).

Struck on underside of basket bottom.

Form

By the 1760s table baskets made from a
single sheet of metal, with pierced sides, cast rim,
and cast base rings, were becoming markedly
smaller than during the preceding decade.

Increased demand for this useful serving
piece combined with the ready availability of bulk
silver wire to produce a shift in style to the more
economical mass-produced wire basket. By 1755
this new form had eliminated the competition of
the earlier hand-worked pierced basket.

---

1. Penzer, 1954, p. 59.

1. See the fruit baskets and centerpieces by Storr in the
    Duke of Wellington service, Apsley House, London, re-
    produced in Penzer, 1954, pl. XXXIII.

Thematic decorations (wheat, fruit, etc.) adorned the silver basket soon after it first appeared as part of domestic plate. Often, though not inevitably, these decorations denoted the intended purpose of the commission when the shape of the actual container did not: wheat sheaves for bread baskets, fruit and flowers for dessert baskets. However, these thematic elements were rarely so integral to the design as in this Storr basket. Far from the cheap wire baskets that proliferated in the second half of the eighteenth century, this heavy sculptural creation blends traditional basketry techniques with complex castings to give the naturalistic appearance of woven wheat. The deep, curving, open casting of the outer rim of wheat tassels is a spectacular example of the metal caster's art. Both structurally sound and decorative, this rim establishes the wheat theme that is continued in the woven sides. The heavy cast foot ring also simulates wheat stalks that have been both woven and braided, while the gilding further reinforces the wheatlike effect.

Although Storr produced other baskets of similar construction,[1] they are only secondary elements within larger compositions and lack the sculptural qualities seen here.

22. Tea Urn, 1802

Silver gilt
Extreme height: 19¼ in. (49 cm.)
Extreme length: 14¾ in. (37.5 cm.)
Urn height: 12½ in. (31.7 cm.)
Urn width: 8¼ in. (21 cm.)
Stand height: 7½ in. (19 cm.)
Stand length: 9 in. (22.9 cm.)
Stand width: 7 in. (17.8 cm.)
Total weight: 218 oz., 6 dwt.
(6,789.586 grams)
Urn: 153 oz., 12 dwt. (4,776.807 grams)
Stand: 65 oz., 4 dwt. (2,026.954 grams)
m. 77.2.12a–e

Hallmarks

Storr's fourth mark.

Lion passant gardant (Sterling Standard).

Crowned leopard head (London assay).

Capital *G* (letter date for 1802).

Monarch's head (George III) (duty stamp).

Struck outside on bottom of urn and on base of stand.

Maker's mark struck on inner rim of lid.

Maker's mark, lion passant gardant, monarch's head, and letter date struck on lid of ingot chamber.

Applied Crest

Vane crest for William Harry, third Earl of Darlington.

On a wreath, a cubit arm in armour grasping a sword Proper.

An earl's coronet above.

Storr

In its reliance on simple shapes and restrained decorative bands, this large oval urn on stand demonstrates the nature of Storr's early style. Horizontal bands of diagonal fluting and braiding relieve the highly polished surface and focus attention on the twin snakes that form the handle. This is the restrained elegance of early English neoclassicism. Storr produced a teakettle (on a stand with a lamp) with nearly the same simple classic design,[1] but it is of circular shape and rests on a low flaring stand raised on winged lion paws. The unusual stand supporting the Gilbert urn carries, in a rather self-conscious way, a three-dimensional realization of the Vane crest, placed in the spot previously reserved for spirit burners (indicating the newness of the Wadham system). Below the low-domed lid of the urn is a second lid, covering the chamber for the heavy iron ingot of Wadham's patented heating device.

Form

The tea urn, a standing hot water container with spigot, apparently evolved from the wine fountain at the beginning of the 1700s. But early examples had no provision for keeping water hot, limiting their value to the rapidly growing tea-drinking cult in England. Burners, like those that heated teakettles (cat. nos. 4, 9, 10), exuded unpleasant odors or required expensive fumeless fuels. Consequently, they had declined in popularity by the late 1760s (though they continued to be made well into the nineteenth century), when charcoal burners became the favored heating device. The hot charcoal was placed in a central well and heated the surrounding liquid by radiation and conduction.

By 1774 John Wadham had patented in London the heating device used in this urn by Storr. It featured a reusable heated iron bar placed in a central core to heat the liquid in the urn without emitting any foul-smelling fumes or spilling any flammable liquids.

Urns became so popular in the late 1700s that they fostered a new form of furniture: the urn table. This small-topped stand held the urn at the proper height for use by a seated hostess. Usually a small slide pulled out from the top to hold a cup or teapot for refilling or to support a small bowl to catch any drips from the spigot.

1. Penzer, 1954, p. 114, pl. XVIII.

23. Set of Four Soup Tureens, 1806–7

Total weight of set: 1,686 oz., 13 dwt.
(52,445.651 grams)

Large Pair
Extreme height: 17½ in. (44.4 cm.)
Extreme width: 18½ in. (47 cm.)
Diameter of tureen: 12⅝ in. (32.1 cm.)
Diameter of stand: 17½ in. (44.4 cm.)
Total weight: 520 oz., 8 dwt.
(16,187.279 grams)
1. Weight of tureen (with attached stand): 460
oz., 19 dwt. (14,337.507 grams)
1. Weight of lid: 59 oz., 9 dwt. (1,849.772
grams)
Total weight: 518 oz., 12 dwt. (16,130.579
grams)
2. Weight of tureen (with attached stand): 453
oz., 18 dwt. (14,117.80 grams)
2. Weight of lid: 64 oz., 14 dwt. (2,012.779
grams)

Small Pair
Extreme height: 15½ in. (39.2 cm.)
Extreme width: 16 in. (40.6 cm.)
Diameter of tureen: 10½ in. (26.7 cm.)
Diameter of stand: 15 in. (38.1 cm.)
Total weight: 323 oz., 7 dwt.
(10,056.81 grams)
3. Weight of tureen (with attached stand): 284
oz., 3 dwt. (8,837.80 grams)
3. Weight of lid: 39 oz., 4 dwt.
(1,219.01 grams)
Total weight: 323 oz., 16 dwt.
(10,070.983 grams)
4. Weight of tureen (with attached stand): 283
oz., 18 dwt. (8,830.714 grams)
4. Weight of lid: 39 oz., 18 dwt.
(1,240.269 grams)
m. 75.135.48a–l

Hallmarks

Storr's fourth mark.

Lion passant gardant (Sterling Standard).

Crowned leopard head (London assay).

2: Capital *L* (letter date for 1806).

1, 3, 4: Capital *M* (letter date for 1807).

Monarch's head (George III) (duty stamp).

Struck on plain bowl near handle and under each
stand.

Maker's mark, lion passant gardant, and letter
date struck on rim of lid.

Engraved Crest

On a ducal coronet, a crowned lion statant gardant
with the Garter.

A ducal coronet above.

Storr

continued

Storr

Form

After being produced in myriad rococo sculptural forms during the 1740s, soup tureens were simplified under the influence of the Adam brothers' neoclassicism. Robert Adam, a designer who planned not only the house, the room, the table, but also the silver from which his client was to dine, introduced the single-footed boat-shaped tureen on oval stand, which was to persist into the early nineteenth century. These tureens were often produced in sets with four or more smaller sauce tureens. The characteristic small-scale linear decoration applied to and chased on this style tureen was similar to that used by the Adams in designs for ceiling plaster and even carpets, a style based in part on decorations found in the new excavations at Pompeii and Herculaneum.[1]

By the first decade of the nineteenth century, massiveness was the primary quality sought in good silver, affecting both form and decorative detail. As a result, little remains of the Adams influence in the tureens seen here except the single stems and the boat-shaped silhouette.

The Battle of the Nile (1 August 1798), at which Admiral Nelson defeated Bonaparte's fleet, re-established the English presence in the Mediterranean; made Nelson a national hero; and introduced Egyptian themes into the neoclassical style of the early nineteenth century. Europe had little direct knowledge (either historical or artistic) of Egypt before 1798, although practitioners of the neoclassical style had found some Egyptian examples in Rome (e.g., the Temple of Isis) and dilettantes collected Egyptian artifacts as exotic curiosities. Not until 1802 was a first-hand account of Egypt available, in Baron Denon's *Voyage dans la Basse et la Haute Égypte.* By that time England and the Continent were experiencing a brief infatuation with all things Egyptian.

Thomas Hope did more than anyone to popularize the Egyptian taste in England, urging "young artists never to adopt, except from motives more weighty than mere novelty, the Egyptian style of ornament."[2] By 1807, Hope was decrying the decay of this style, evidenced by the "Modern imitations of these wonders of antiquity, composed of lath and plaster, of callico and of paper... which can only excite ridicule and contempt."[3] From Hope's book, in which he recorded his outstanding Egyptian collection and the designs of his home in Duchess St., London, which he remodeled for it, we can see that his collection included numerous examples from the antique that inspired both the neoclassical and Egyptian styles (including at least two small versions of the Artemis of Ephesus).[4]

To celebrate Nelson's victory at the Battle of the Nile, the Company of Merchants commissioned a commemorative cup, which Paul Storr executed. The Battle of the Nile Cup, presented to the Rt. Hon. Rear Admiral Horatio Nelson in 1799, varies only slightly from Storr's neoclassical style, with token references to Egypt seen in the low-relief crocodiles on the lid. The handles, however, are more fully Egyptianate: curving cornucopia from which issue winged sphinxes, draped in classical tunics and wearing the Egyptian *nemset* headdress. These handles are the prototypes of those on the Gilbert tureens. The remaining decoration is Roman in inspiration, with waterleaves, beading, anthemia, etc.

In 1803 Storr created a set of four large and four small tureens for a royal commission.[5] This set, on which the Gilbert tureens were patterned, shows little advance in accurate knowledge of Egypt, exemplifying the neo-Egyptian taste that Hope had decried. Both sets of tureens have cast handles that synthesize the cornucopia-sphinx seen on the Nile Cup with the many-breasted Ephesian Artemis. Other sphinxes appear in low relief on the sides of the tureen bowls. In large panels above them are depicted various fanciful scenes of sacrificial rites, concocted by a nineteenth-century designer from Greco-Roman examples. The result is a static relief that resembles those seen on many Wedgwood pieces. Like the Nile Cup, the Egyptian motifs on these tureens are interspersed with elements from Storr's standard decorative vocabulary: twined snakes form the lid handle, waterleaves border the rim of the lid.

The stands that support the Gilbert tureens are also cross-cultural composites. The wide decorative borders are derived from similar borders on a pair of tureen stands by the Parisian silversmith Henri Auguste. Storr directly adapted the alternating square and round rosettes on these 1787 stands (which were in the Royal Collection at the time the 1803 tureens were commissioned), although considerably reducing their scale. The feet of the Gilbert stands are typical Storr neoclassical creations, with lion paws, volutes, and honeysuckle fillets. The same style foot can be seen in plates XLI, XLIX, and LII, of Thomas Hope's 1807 style book.

1. Horace Walpole belittled the Adams' style as "gingerbread and snippets of embroidery."
2. Hope, p. 131.
3. Ibid.
4. Ibid, pl. X.
5. Jones, 1911, p. 31.

24. Salver or Tray, 1808

Silver gilt
Extreme height: 4 in. (10.2 cm.)
Extreme length: 37 in. (94 cm.)
Extreme width: 24½ in. (62.2 cm.)
Total weight: 407 oz., 4 dwt.
(12,664.916 grams)
m. 77.1.7

Hallmarks

Storr's sixth mark.

Lion passant gardant (Sterling Standard).

Crowned leopard head (London assay).

Capital *N* (letter date for 1808).

Monarch's head (George III) (duty stamp).

Struck underneath on flat surface.

Engraved Arms and Crest

The achievement of Baron Monson, probably for
Frederick John Monson (1809–1841), fifth Baron
Monson.

Or two chevrons Gules.

Above the shield a baron's coronet and Peer's helm
with mantling.

On a wreath a lion Proper supporting a column Or
(crest of Monson).

Supporters: on a compartment a lion Or and a
griffin wings addorsed Argent beaked and armed
Azure.

Both collared and chained[1] Azure, on the collar
three crescents Or.

Motto: *Prest pour mon pais* ("Ready for my
country").

The style of this engraving and the positions of the
supporters suggest that the engraving was added
in the 1830s, probably about 1832, the year of
Frederick John Monson's marriage.

Form

An outgrowth of the oval salver of the early
eighteenth century, this shape (with handles at
both ends) appeared as early as 1755 as serving
stands for large tureens. By 1775 oval trays (with
handles cast as integral parts of the cast rims) were
commonly accepted as independent serving pieces.
As with most silver serving items, the oval tray
increased in size near the turn of the nineteenth
century.

According to the tenth Baron Monson, the fourth lord (1785–1809), rich and in the flush of youth, had had great plans for entertaining at both his London house and his country seat in Lincolnshire. It was he who reputedly ordered from Storr this oval serving tray as well as an exceptional, two-tiered centerpiece. But the lord died prematurely, at the age of twenty-four, within a year of receiving his domestic plate.[2]

The nineteenth-century fashion for lavishly engraved arms caught up to the tray with the fifth Earl of Monson, who had the large arms engraved as we now see them in about 1832. Impressive as the crest is, it is nevertheless dominated by the wide cast oak-leaf border and voluted handles. The applied cast masks on the handles bear a striking resemblance to the comic and tragic masks of Silenus engraved in Thomas Hope's early treatise on the neoclassical taste, *Household Furniture and Interior Decoration* (London, 1807).

1. Variation for collared and lined as recorded.
2. Penzer, 1954, p. 128.

25. Jug on Stand, 1809

Extreme height: 11⅛ in. (28.2 cm.)
Jug height: 8½ in. (21.6 cm.)
Jug diameter: 6¼ in. (15.9 cm.)
Stand height: 4⅛ in. (10.5 cm.)
Total weight: 55 oz., 9 dwt. (1,725.745 grams)
Jug: 31 oz., 3 dwt. (969.181 grams)
Stand: 24 oz., 6 dwt. (756.564 grams)
m. 75.135.41a, b

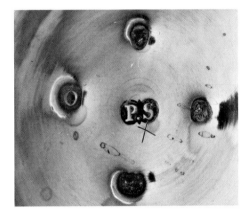

Hallmarks

Storr's sixth mark.

Lion passant gardant (Sterling Standard).

Crowned leopard head (London assay).

Capitol *O* (letter date for 1809).

Monarch's head (George III) (duty stamp).

Struck on concave bottom of jug and under base of stand.

Small maker's mark, lion passant gardant, and *O* letter date struck inside lid.

Lion passant gardant and *O* letter date struck inside burner lid.

Form

Jugs have been produced in silver since the mid-sixteenth century, though few early examples exist. The ewer and flagon were more popular vessels for the same function (holding and serving a variety of liquids) until the advent of "Turkey Coffee" in the mid-eighteenth century. From this time jugs were used equally as containers for hot water and as coffee "pots." The wide pouring spout and ability to hold heat, particularly when coupled with a spirit lamp, fitted the jug for many uses. When the silver coffeepot ceased to be popular in the 1790s,[1] it is certain that much of its function was assumed by the jug on stand.

This pyriform jug on stand is one of many produced by Storr in the first quarter of the nineteenth century. Its design is based on drawings made by the Adam brothers (Robert and James) in the third quarter of the eighteenth century.[2] The many versions by Storr that survive with only minimal variations in decorative treatment testify to the popularity of this design. This particular example is most notable for the addition of a fluted band around the waist of the jug and the cast winged serpent head and tail, which serve as sockets for the ivory handle.

No strainer is provided under the low-domed lid, indicating that this jug was probably commissioned as a hot water container.

1. Clayton, p. 171.
2. Ibid., p. 11.

Storr

Silver gilt and cut glass
Extreme height: 15⅞ in. (40.3 cm.)
Stand height: 13½ in. (34.3 cm.)
Width of base: 10 in. (25.4 cm.)
Diameter of bowl: 6 in. (15.2 cm.)
Total weight: 172 oz., 6 dwt.
(5,357.961 grams)
m. 75.135.38a, b

The three figures on this stand represent bacchantes, or priests of Bacchus, wearing the *peplos* (a woman's garment worn in Greece during the fifth century B.C.). The figures each hold two forms of the *thyrsus,* the staff carried by Bacchus and his votaries.

Storr produced at least two versions of this tall dessert stand. This example is easily differentiated from those in the Wellington service[1] by the erect stance of the caryatid figures: though produced the same year as this stand, the Wellington versions have shorter figures with bent left knees.

The most noticeable characteristic distinguishing the Gilbert stand from those in the Wellington service is the inclusion of a cut-glass dish; the Wellington stands all have wire baskets with glass liners. The flanged lip (apparently original) just above the decorative top ring of this stand, not present in the basket version, indicates that the Gilbert stand was intended to carry a glass container. The seven-lobed cut-glass dish is a late nineteenth-century replacement.

Hallmarks

Storr's sixth mark.

Lion passant gardant (Sterling Standard).

Capital *P* (letter date for 1810).

Monarch's head (George III) (duty stamp).

Struck under base and sub-base.

Maker's mark, lion passant gardant, and monarch's head struck inside top platform and on back (costume fold) of each figure.

Maker's mark and lion passant gardant struck on each staff near hand.

Underside of base struck with inscription: *Rundell Bridge et Rundell aurifices Regis et Principis Wallae Londini* and with pattern or catalog number: 466.

Form

Although mentioned in Elizabethan inventories, no dessert stands survive from before the 1630s. The term was arbitrarily applied to most early examples since they were simply variations of the central-footed salver. By 1700 the dessert stand was replaced by the low strawberry dish (see cat. no. 3), and later in the century, baskets and epergnes were favored for serving desserts, sweetmeats, and fruits. The tall branched epergne reached its height of popularity in the rococo and Adam periods of the mid- and late 1700s, with the revived vogue for tall central silver pieces to adorn the dinner table.

With the neoclassical movement of the early nineteenth century, the true dessert stand again came into style. These stands were made in sets of two and four, as secondary or supplementary pieces to the centerpiece on the long dining tables of the Regency period where they would remain as decoration throughout the meal.

1. Penzer, 1954, p. 144.

Silver gilt
Extreme height: 28⅞ in. (73.3 cm.)
Width of base: 10 in. (25.4 cm.)
Extreme width: 20 in. (50.7 cm.)
Diameter of dish: 11 in. (28 cm.)
Total weight: 504 oz., 14 dwt.
(15,698.259 grams)
m. 77.2.14

Hallmarks

Storr's eighth mark.

Lion passant gardant (Sterling Standard).

Crowned leopard head (London assay).

Capital *S* (letter date for 1813).

Monarch's head (George III) (duty stamp).

Struck under base and on each wax pan.

Each socket struck with maker's mark, lion passant gardant, and monarch's head.

Each cast lion struck with maker's mark, lion passant gardant, and monarch's head.

continued

Engraved Arms

The seal of the City of Newcastle-under-Lyme, Staffordshire, in decorative scrollwork.

Arms of Bootle-Wilbraham for Edward Bootle-Wilbraham (1771–1853), Member of Parliament for Newcastle-under-Lyme, 1796–1812 (later created Baron Skelmersdale, 1828), with quarterings, impaling Taylor of Bifrons (for Elizabeth, daughter of Reverend Edward Taylor of Bifrons, in Patrixbourne, Kent).

Quarterly of twelve:

1 and 12, quarterly 1 and 4, Gules a chevron and three combs Argent (Bootle).

2 and 3, Argent three bars wavy Azure (Wilbraham).

2, Azure two bars Argent, on a canton Sable a wolf's head erased Argent (Wilbraham).

3, Azure two bars and in chief two cinquefoils Argent (Venables).

4, Gules a fess and three lozenges Argent (Crossley).

5, Argent a cross patonce between four martlets and a label Gules (Golbourne).

6, Argent on a fess Gules three molets Argent (Clive) (variant—the molets should be Or).

7, Ermine on a bend cotised Gules three crescents Argent (Huxley) (variant—crescents should be Or).

8, Azure a chevron and three tau crosses Argent (not recorded, possibly for Tewe).

9, Sable three garbs Argent (Styche) (variant— garbs should be Or).

10, Sable a lion rampant and three crosses formy fitchy Argent (variant—lion and crosses should be Or) (possibly for King).

11, Quarterly Argent and Sable four cocks countercolored (unidentified coat in Creswick's roll of 1445–46).

Lord Skelmersdale's father married Mary, co-heiress of Robert Bootle, and took the name in addition to his own. The quarterings of Venables, Crossley, Golbourne, and Clive represent alliances that the Wilbrahams had established by the 1200s. The arms of Huxley, Tewe, and Styche were added in 1619 when Thomas Wilbraham married the heiress Rachel Clive. The last two quarterings have not been recorded in pedigrees.

Engraved Inscription

Rundell Bridge et Rundell aurifices Regis et Principis Wallae Londini.

Form

With the use of a large standing salt as the focal point of a table in the early sixteenth century, the tradition of tall silver table decorations began. As salt became more plentiful, it diminished in symbolic importance, and arrangements of fresh fruit replaced it as a symbol of abundance and hospitality.

Among the new forms developed in the eighteenth century to display fruit, flowers, and sweetmeats were the many-armed epergne, the centerpiece, and the dessert stand. The centerpiece, consisting of a single-dished container raised on a central stem or four feet, had developed as a distinct form by 1730. With the neoclassical movement of the early nineteenth century, the centerpiece, more suited to the new style, supplanted the epergne as table decoration. At this point, centerpiece design shifted in emphasis and its function as container became less important than its role as table sculpture.

Unlike Storr's later decorative centerpieces,[1] this early example displays a massive, cohesive design. The concave triangular base, sculptural crouching lions, and concave pyramidal sub-base provide a secure foundation for the stem, unlike some later examples in which the small single base is inadequate, visually and physically, to balance the reach of the candle arms. The bold central stem springs from an acanthus-leaf calyx to support the reeded central bowl and spiraling branches. The design of this centerpiece is indirectly based[2] on a pair of antique marble candelabra in the Vatican Museum,[3] which were popular with tourists and even reproduced in plaster as souvenirs. Piranesi included engravings of them in his *Vasi, candelabri . . .* of 1778, but Storr's design was most likely based on drawings[4] and casts[5] from Charles Heathcote Tatham, an architect and purchasing agent. Tatham, who published *Designs for Ornamental Plate* in 1806, is known to have also provided drawings for Rundell, Bridge & Rundell.[6] This centerpiece is only one of the many silver and silver-gilt versions based on his drawings.

1. One of a pair of silver-gilt centerpieces, 1816, repr. in *Art at Auction, 1967–68*, p. 365, and a centerpiece/epergne, 1816, repr. in *Antiques,* CI, February 1972, p. 276, demonstrate the wide variety of compositions that grew from Storr's earlier creations.
2. *The Age of Neo-classicism*, p. 767, entry no. 1638, pl. 134.
3. Ameling, nos. 412–13, pp. 627–36, pl. 60–1, and Udy, p. 275, ill. 7.
4. Udy, p. 276, ill. 8.
5. Tatham had procured the casts for the architect Henry Holland. William Riedeur in the *Age of Neo-classicism,* entry no. 1638, suggests that Holland's interest was in producing a mahogany version, possibly for the Prince of Wales' Carlton House, which Holland was remodeling.
6. Penzer, 1954, p. 19.

28. Warwick Vase, 1814

Silver gilt
Extreme height: 17⅝ in. (44.8 cm.)
Extreme width: 14¼ in. (36.2 cm.)
Vase height: 9⁹/₁₆ in. (24.3 cm.)
Diameter at lip: 10½ in. (26.7 cm.)
Base height: 8⅝ in. (22 cm.)
Base width: 8¼ in. (21 cm.)
Total weight: 283 oz., 5 dwt.
(8,809.452 grams)
m. 75.135.37a, b

Hallmarks

Storr's eighth mark.

Lion passant gardant (Sterling Standard).

Crowned leopard head (London assay).

Capital *T* (letter date for 1814).

Monarch's head (George III) (duty stamp).

Engraved Arms

Quarterly Macgregor and Grant, with the crest and motto of Macgregor matriculated for James Macgregor, M. D., in Lyon Court, Edinburgh, 1811.

Quarterly 1 and 4, Argent on a mount a fir tree Vert over all a sword in bend Azure the point touching and antique crown in chief Gules (Macgregor).

2 and 3, Gules three antique crowns Or (Grant).

On a wreath, a lion's head erased crowned with an antique crown proper (crest of Macgregor).

Motto (above the crest in Scottish practice): *Srioghal Mo Dhream.*

Engraved Inscription

CUI DENIQUE SACROS HYGENIAE FONTES APE RIRE

ATQUE ARTIS MEDENDI DIVINAE STUDIA

Viin aennulam ingennas apud Scientias eliciendo

PROMOVERE FELICITER OMNINO CONTIGERIT;

HOCCE MONUMENTUM, QUALE QUALE PIGNUS!

SUMMAE IN DUCEM SUUM DIGNISSIMUM

OBSERVATIAE

SACRUM AC PERĒNNE VULT

STATUS MAJOR NOSOCOMIENSIS

WELLINGTONIANUS
ANNO DOM. 1814
JACOBO McGRIGOR EQUITI M.D.
COLL. REG. MED. EDIN. SOC.
SOCIET. REG. EDIN. SOD.

Nosocomiorum Regalium Inspectori Generali

VIRO ADMODUM INSIGNITO
SIVE ACUMEN INGENII NATIVUM RESPICIAS
SIVE STRENUAM ILLAM ATQUE INDEFESSAM
MUNERIBUS INSPECTORIIS NAVATAM OPERAM
LONGE LATEQUE FUNGENDIS

Non Bono solum Publico cum integritate prope singulgri

VERUMENTIAM SOCIIS SUIS COOPER ANTIBUS
COMITATE QUADAM ET BENIGNITATE PROPRIA
NUMQUAM NON CONSULUERIT[1]

Form

Probably no single object represents the British fascination with the antique better than the Warwick Vase. The fragments of the original large[2] marble vase that gave this shape its name were found by Gavin Hamilton in a lake at Hadrian's Villa north of Rome in 1770. From the fragments Piranesi produced his engraved concept of the vase in 1778,[3] guaranteeing its fame and ultimate popularity as a decorative form. Work to restore the marble vase was later begun under the sponsorship of Sir William Hamilton, already renowned as a collector of Greek antiquities. He provided the necessary three hundred pounds for reconstruction of the vase, restoring the missing parts and providing the square plinth on which it rests. This generous sponsorship was in fact a speculation on his part, an effort to produce a salable commodity which he speedily offered to the British Museum. The museum declined. Sir William then persuaded his nephew George Greville, the Earl of Warwick, to purchase the monumental piece. The original vase can be seen today at Warwick Castle, displayed in the fine greenhouse pavilion that the earl had built for it.[4]

Various efforts have been made to produce accurate facsimile copies of the Warwick Vase. The first was an attempt in 1813 by Rundell, Bridge & Rundell to make a full-scale copy in silver for Lord Lonsdale. Storr probably worked on this aborted project, producing some of the molds and familiarizing himself with the restored original; he had previously (as early as 1810) re-created the vase from the Piranesi engraving.

In the first half of the nineteenth century, the Warwick Vase shape was reproduced in pottery, porcelain, marble, iron, copper, Sheffield plate, and silver. These versions served as presentation cups, ice pails, soup tureens, and teapots, to mention only a few. One of the best-known variations of the Warwick Vase is the presentation cup trophy known as the Ascot Cup, now in the Art Institute of Chicago, on which Storr substituted equestrian heads for human ones.

Of the many versions of the Warwick Vase produced in the first half of the nineteenth century, this is one of the most successful. It is strictly a presentation piece. The base is a slightly slenderized version of the original and bears inscriptions in Latin, as does that created for Sir William. From the crisp casting and chasing of the vine handles and masks it can be appreciated that Storr had recently made molds from the original.

1. The Latin in this inscription is a modern fabrication and makes no sense.
2. Height: 61 in., diameter: 70 in.
3. *Vasi, Candelabri, Cippi*, Rome, 1778.
4. Penzer, 1955–56, entire article.

29. Punch Ladle, 1814

Length: 19¼ in. (48.9 cm.)
Width of bowl: 5⅞ in. (15 cm.)
Total weight: 23 oz., 6 dwt.
(724.671 grams)
m. 77.2.15

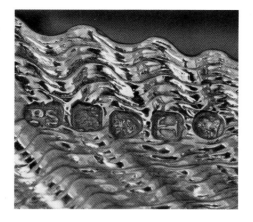

Hallmarks

Storr's ninth mark.

Lion passant gardant (Sterling Standard).

Crowned leopard head (London assay).

Upper-case *T* (letter date for 1814).

Monarch's head (George III) (duty stamp).

Struck outside on top of shell.

Form

From the 1760s ladle bowls took many shapes; even coconut and sea shells were mounted in silver to serve this purpose, and these exotic combinations inspired contemporary and later versions entirely in silver. Large-scale ladles in these natural forms were favored for corporate or civic plate in the early years of the nineteenth century. At the same time, the bowls of domestic ladles diminished in size, reflecting the increased alcoholic content of the beverages they were used to serve.

With the prosperity of the early nineteenth century, cities began to build up their corporate plate, and large punch bowls with ladles proved especially useful items for civic functions. The pair of large punch bowls that our ladle originally accompanied bear the corporate seal of the city of Dover. All bowls and ladles by Storr bear the letter date for 1814 (the punch bowls also carry the inscription for Rundell, Bridge & Rundell and were presented by A. Peter Factor, Esq.). Even though commissioned at the same time, the ladles do not actually match, although their decoration is similar. The bowls are banded about the waist with a wide frieze of roses, thistles, and shamrocks (symbolizing England, Scotland, and Ireland, respectively). About the cast rims of the bowls are acanthus and shell motifs.

Our ladle is an extraordinarily sculptural piece of silver. The intricately cast clam shell (the *Hippopus hippopus*) that forms the bowl of the ladle rests snugly in the voluted end of the curving handle, as though cushioned in the petals of a blossom. The arched reeded stem is balanced at the other end with acanthus leaves and a waterleaf-bud finial.

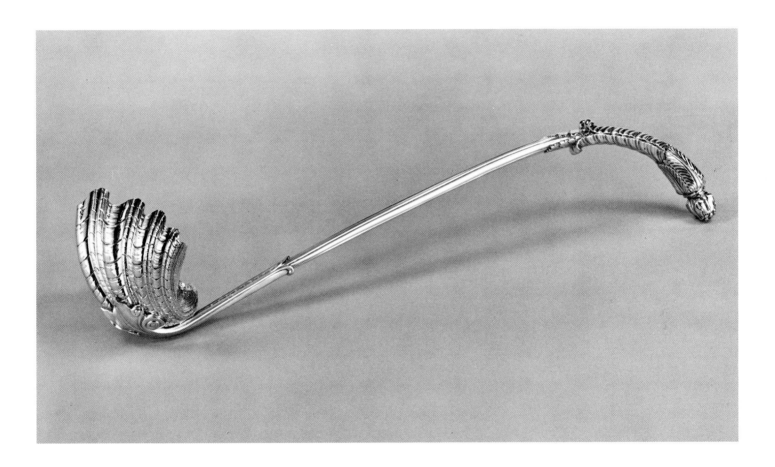

30. Set of Four Candlesticks, 1815

Silver gilt
Extreme height: 9¼ in. (23.5 cm.)
Width: 5½ in. (14 cm.)
Total weight: 107 oz., 17 dwt.
(3,355.813 grams)
1: 26 oz., 11 dwt. (825.665 grams)
2: 27 oz., 3 dwt. (845.155 grams)
3: 27 oz., 4 dwt. (846.926 grams)
4: 26 oz., 19 dwt. (838.067 grams)
m. 77.1.5a–h

Hallmarks

Storr's eighth mark.

Lion passant gardant (Sterling Standard).

Capital *U* (letter date for 1815).

Monarch's head (George III) (duty stamp).

Struck on outer rim of base.

Maker's mark struck on top of each wax pan.

Form

Like many pieces produced by Storr in the second decade of the nineteenth century, these candlesticks reflect a return to earlier forms. Most popular in the 1730s–50s, the baluster-form stick was produced in many variations on both a plain style and an elaborate rococo one. Developing from the rococo sticks of the late forties and fifties, and in part a revival of the late seventeenth-century style, figurative sticks became most popular in the 1770s. These highly sculptural forms varied from caryatid figures that blended architectural elements with the human form to complex castings that represented the human body as a fully rounded sculptural stem, supporting—only incidentally—a socket for candles.

The classical Adam style replaced this elaborate sculptural style and dominated candlesticks through the end of the eighteenth century. A drawing by the Adam brothers from about 1764 (now in the Sir John Soane Museum, London)[1] best illustrates this shape. A tall slender baluster, it can be seen as the inspiration for so many simpler sticks later produced in the same style (particularly by Matthew Boulton with whom Robert Adam is known to have collaborated at his Soho works).[2] By the end of the eighteenth century much of the more decorative vocabulary of classicism had disappeared. In its place, simple vase shapes with flattened fluting (much easier and more economical to produce) became the dominant style.

With the Regency period, opulence was again in vogue. It manifested itself first in the extravagant, expansive scale of the neoclassical style (see cat. no. 36), then in the lush opulence seen here that heralded the return to the rococo style.

Engraved Crest

On a wreath, an eagle rising.

Unidentified.

Struck Inscription

Rundell Bridge et Rundell aurifices Regis et Principis Wallae Regent.

Numbers 1–4 struck on sockets and wax pans.

1. Clayton, p. 43, ill. 79.
2. Edwards and Ramsey, ed., IV, p. 70, and Judith Banister, "Silver Candlesticks and Candelabra," *Antique Collector,* April 1976, p. 36.
3. Penzer, 1954, p. 174, pl. XLVIII, and Oman, 1965, ill. 200.

In describing an identical pair of candlesticks now in the Victoria and Albert Museum,[3] N. M. Penzer points out that this design is a stylistic anachronism. The shouldered silhouette of the shaft was favored at the end of the seventeenth century. The decoration applied to the shaft is in the Adam style of 1770–90. The nearly square base is in de Lamerie's rococo style of 1736–42. All from quite separate styles, the elements were brought together by Storr with carefully controlled proportions and thereby saved from banal eclecticism.

The bases are examples of the decorative allegories that became increasingly important in the early nineteenth century. At the corners are applied cast human masks, each adorned with symbols that Penzer identifies as the Seasons but which also can be identified with individual gods: shells and water (winter or Neptune); flowers (spring or Flora); fruit (summer or Pomona); and leaves and grapes (fall or Bacchus).

By the mid- to late teens Storr seems less involved with the story-telling aspect of neoclassical decoration and more concerned with the development of an eclectic style. These candlesticks, in their focus on rich surface decoration borrowed freely from other times, are forerunners of the all-engulfing Victorian romanticism.

31. Soy Frame, 1816

Silver with cut-glass bottles
Height: 9½ in. (24.2 cm.)
Extreme length: 11½ in. (29.2 cm.)
Width: 8 in. (20.3 cm.)
Total weight (without bottles): 53 oz., 6 dwt.
(1,658.417 grams)
m. 75.135.47a–i

Hallmarks

Storr's eighth mark.

Lion passant gardant (Sterling Standard).

Crowned leopard head (London assay).

Lower-case *a* (letter date for 1816).

Monarch's head (George III) (duty stamp).

Struck under base of frame near rim.

Form

A smaller version of the cruet (or oil and
vinegar frame, introduced in 1706), the soy frame
was intended as a supplement for that two-bottle,
three-caster server. Appearing after 1760, the soy
frame usually held six bottles—attesting to the
demand for pungent sauces during a period of
little or no technology in food preservation. From
bottle tickets (silver labels hung around the neck
of each bottle) it is known that soy frames carried
soy sauce, ketchup, lemon vinegar, pickles,
"Kyan" (cayenne), anchovy, cherokee, quin, tarra-
gon, chili, and cavice sauces, as well as a commer-
cial product popular from 1815 called Wood's fish
sauce.[1] In some forms the soy frame included a
mustard pot (now incorporated in modern English
cruets) as well as pepper and cayenne casters.[2]

1. These caused James Russell Lowell to comment in *The
   Bigelow Papers* that:
   "of all the sarse that I can call to mind
   England doos make the most unpleasant kind."
2. John Salter, "Discovering Silver Condiment Labels,"
   Country Life, CLX, no. 4135, 30 September 1976, pp.
   896–98.
3. Edwards and Ramsey, ed., III, pp. 76, 78, pl. 41.

Storr

This small soy frame, retaining its original four bottles and stoppers, displays a large-scale decorative scheme that indicates it is based on the design, and some castings, of a larger cruet. The large handles at either end of the base, the shell-scrolled feet, the fluting of the outer rim, the flat acanthus brackets supporting the upper ring, and the heart-shaped handle are all of larger proportions than the delicacy of the cut-glass bottles would dictate.

The design of the silver frame shows neoclassical motifs beginning to thicken into florid Victorian decor. The small bottles are raised on turned bases, with bodies cut in an over-all field known as "strawberry diamond," popular in the early nineteenth century.[3] The silver collars on each bottle are decorated with low-relief anthemion forms and scroll outward to provide two pouring spouts.

32. Pair of Four-Light Candelabra, 1816

Silver gilt
Height: 28⅞ in. (73.3 cm.)
Reach: 14 in. (35.6 cm.)
Width of base: 10 in. (25.4 cm.)
Total weight: 408 oz., 6 dwt.
(1,270.352 grams)
m. 77.2.16a–j

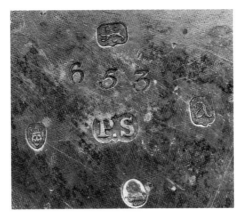

Storr's eighth mark.

Lion passant gardant (Sterling Standard).

Crowned leopard head (London assay).

Lower-case *a* (letter date for 1816).

Monarch's head (George III) (duty stamp).

Struck under bases.[1]

Form

Candelabra were common in all popular metals from the fourteenth to the sixteenth centuries. The earliest dated silver candelabra, or "branch candlesticks," still extant are considered to be the pair at Welbeck Abbey, Nottinghamshire (formerly owned by the Duke of Portland), dated 1697. Because existing silver sticks were often updated with the addition of branches, it is exceptional to find early matching pairs before the mid-1700s. At that point candelabra became the most popular lighting device and were manufactured in sets.

Before 1770 the stems carried two branching arms, each holding a single candle socket and joined at center with a finial plug. This central plug fitted into the candle socket of the stem, permitting optional use with one or two lights. After 1770 the central position between the arms carried a third socket, replacing the finial and providing more light. As a further option, with some sets of candelabra a finial stopper was provided for this central socket. This flexibility in candelabra design indicates the extreme care and discretion used in the eighteenth century with expensive candles. By the early nineteenth century less caution seems to have been exerted in the use of candles, and multi-armed candelabra were the accepted form.

Engraved Crests

On a wreath, a lion rampant Argent holding a shield of the arms.

A baron's coronet above.

Engraved on the wax pans of each socket.

The arms and crest of Foley of Kidderminster (with the variant of quatrefoils in place of cinquefoils), which were granted after the second baron's death in 1776 to a cousin, Baron Foley, Lord Lieutenant of Worcester.

Applied Cast Arms

Achievement of Foley of Kidderminster.

Argent a fess engrailed between three quatrefoils (variant for cinquefoils) a border engrailed Sable.

Above a shield a baron's coronet.

Supporters: two lions Argent semy of quatrefoils (variant for cinquefoils) Sable.

Motto: *Ut prosim* ("That I may do good").

Applied to the concave sides of the triangular bases.

This pair of tall four-light candelabra from a set of four are exceptionally refined examples of Storr's craftsmanship and artistry. Created at the height of popularity of the firm of Rundell, Bridge & Rundell, while Storr was a partner there, they illustrate Storr's transitional period of the mid-1810s. In these candelabra he confronted, if did not resolve, the conflict between neoclassicism and the emerging romantic eclecticism. Elements of both styles are distinguishable here. The form and applied acanthus decorations of the triangular bases are holdovers from earlier designs (see cat. no. 27), as are the cycad forms from which the baluster stems rise. The delicately modulated silhouette of the slender shafts is Adamesque in inspiration, although the intricate surface embellishment is Storr's Regency style used in small scale. Even the finely chased, fixed double acanthus scrolled branches are a refinement of an earlier effort,[2] similar to but more finely worked than those used on Storr's large eight-light centerpiece of 1815.

Storr's works subsequent to this period show less of his abilities and reflect the disillusionment with his partners and their production methods that led to his leaving the partnership in 1820.

Storr

1. This pair of silver-gilt candelabra can be identified as part of a set of four from the numerical stamps found on branch ends, nozzles, and wax pans. The fixed scrolling arms are stamped 1, 2, 3, on one candelabrum and 5, 6, 7 on the other. The center nozzles of each, raised on double palm-spray stems, are stamped 13 and 14, respectively. The nozzles and wax pans have been mixed, for from the sequence of the stamps it would appear that the branches, nozzles, and pans of all four candelabra were struck first, in sequence from 1 to 12, then the center stems and their socket stand pans were struck, numbered 13–16.
2. Penzer, 1954, p. 186, pl. LIV.

33. Pair of Covered Entree Dishes, 1816–17

(On single-plated Sheffield warmers by M. R. Boulton Co.)
Extreme height: 11¼ in. (28.6 cm.)
Total weight (without warmers): 165 oz., 9 dwt. (5,145.826 grams)

Covers
Height: 6 in. (15.2 cm.)
Length: 9¼ in. (23.5 cm.)
Width: 7¾ in. (19.7 cm.)
Weight:
1: 52 oz., 4 dwt. (1,622.98 grams)
2: 53 oz., 2 dwt. (1,651.329 grams)

Dishes
Height: 1¾ in. (4.5 cm.)
Length: 11¹/₁₆ in. (28.1 cm.)
Width: 9½ in. (24.1 cm.)
Weight:
1: 30 oz., 1 dwt. (935.517 grams)
2: 30 oz., 2 dwt. (936.0 grams)

Warmers with Water Jackets
Height: 4½ in. (11.4 cm.)
Length: 14⁵/₁₆ in. (36.4 cm.)
Width: 8¾ in. (21.3 cm.)
m. 77.1.2a–h

Hallmarks

Dishes

Storr's eighth mark.

Lion passant gardant (Sterling Standard).

Crowned leopard head (London assay).

Lower-case *a* (letter date for 1816).

Monarch's head (George III) (duty stamp).

Struck on underside of dish edge.

Covers

Storr's ninth mark.

Lion passant gardant (Sterling Standard).

Lower-case *b* (letter date for 1817).

Struck on plain vertical band below rosette frieze.

Engraved Crest on Water Jackets

On a chapeau Gules the brim Ermine, a leopard Or about the neck a crown Argent.

A duke's coronet above.

Engraved Coronet on Dish

A duke's coronet.

Form

Dinner services (plates and serving pieces) reflect better than any other silver the dining customs of the age that produced them. The *average* eighteenth-century silver service contained seventy-two plates, twelve oval dishes in gradated sizes, and four second-course dishes. To these essentials, additional pieces were added to fit the needs of the individual family (e.g., a *mazarine* with strainer for boiled fish, venison dishes, dish covers, and odd-sized covered dishes). Few dish covers survive from before the nineteenth century, though it is known they did exist earlier. Large covered dishes, today called *second-course dishes*, then functioned also as entree dishes. Derived from the chafing dish of the seventeenth and eighteenth centuries, covered dishes were usually produced in sets of four from the 1770s on. The growing tendency, near the end of the eighteenth century, for families to dine privately with only a small serving staff, if any, made the covered dish indispensable.

In the early nineteenth century warmers (spirit lamps, charcoal, or hot irons) and water jackets were added to keep the food warm.

This pair of covered dishes is from a large dinner service owned by the Dukes of Norfolk. Upon succession to the title in 1815, Bernard Edward, the twelfth duke, apparently continued a commission begun by his father.[1] Nearly forty pieces for this service were completed by Storr between 1814 and 1817, each bearing the arms seen here.

Heavy cast gadroon and shell borders (a style used constantly from the mid-eighteenth century) are applied to horizontal rims of these deep rectangular dishes. The complexly designed covers (altered only slightly on all the covered serving pieces in the Norfolk service, regardless of their shape) rise from plain banded rims at the dish to bold half-round quatrefoil borders to richly embellished domes. The elaborate neo-rococo decoration of the domes recalls de Lamerie's style of some seventy-five years earlier with flower and fruit motifs and diapered panels enclosed by leaf and shell scrolls. Applied on an acanthus medallion in a gadrooned frame at the top of each dome is a bold, hollow-cast handle. The boldly cast quatrefoil borders and the lion head and reeded handles identify the covers as nineteenth-century revival regardless of how finely the rococo surface decoration mimics the earlier eighteenth-century style.

The four-legged, single-plated Sheffield warmers by the M. R. Boulton Co., Birmingham,[2] must be considered separately from their sterling covered dishes. Because it required less silver, was structurally sound,[3] and a good conductor, single Sheffield plate was a practical and popular material to construct warmers and other heating items.

The bold swelling forms of these stands, with legs and borders of acanthus leaves and honeysuckle blossoms or anthemia, reflect the rather overblown style. This style, showing the effects of industrial production techniques, indicates a manufacture date after that of the silver dishes they carry.

1. Ronald J. Winokur, "Recent Acquisitions of English Silver," *Detroit Institute Bulletin,* LII, no. 2, March 1973, p. 93.

2. Matthew Boulton (1728–1806), inventor of the Sheffield plating technique, is first known for the production of silver and cut steel buttons and show buckles. He opened his second factory in 1764 where he produced Sheffield plate, sterling, and ormulu. After his death in 1809, the firm continued to produce until 1843, first as M. R. Boulton Co. and later as The Soho Plate Co.

3. The plating process actually strengthens the metal.

continued

Applied Cast Arms on Covers

Quarterly Howard, Brotherton, Warenne, and Mowbray, the supporters and motto of the Duke of Norfolk, for Bernard Edward (Howard), twelfth Duke of Norfolk, 1815 to 1842.

Quarterly 1, Gules on a bend between six cross crosslets fitchy Argent, Shield Or a demi-lion pierced by an arrow in a double tressure counterflory Gules (Howard, with augmentation for Battle of Flodden).

2, Gules three leopards Or a label Argent (Brotherton).

3, Checky Or and Azure (Warenne).

4, Gules a lion rampant Argent (Mowbray).

The shield set on crossed batons for the Earl Marshalship of England and ensigned with the coronet of a duke.

Supporters: a lion and horse Argent, the latter with a sprig of oak in the mouth Proper.

Motto: *Sola virtus invicta* ("Virtue alone is unconquered").

Recorded with three crests, the one shown occurs second. Omission of Howard crest is unusual.

Covered Compote, 1820

Silver, with cut-glass liner
Height: 9 in. (22.8 cm.)
Diameter of lid: 6⅞ in. (17.5 cm.)
Diameter of base: 7⅜ in. (18.7 cm.)
Total weight: 54 oz., 14 dwt.
(1,700.94 grams)
m. 77.1.1a–c

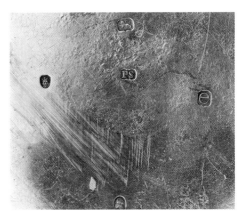

Hallmarks

Storr's ninth mark.

Lion passant gardant (Sterling Standard).

Crowned leopard head (London assay).

Lower-case *e* (letter date for 1820).

Monarch's head (George III) (duty stamp).

Struck center bottom of base and on cast applied grape leaf below ring.

Small maker's mark, lion passant gardant, and letter date struck under lid.

Small maker's mark, lion passant gardant, and monarch's head struck on bolted finial.

Storr

After his severance with Rundell, Bridge & Rundell, and his subsequent move to Harrison Street, Clerkenwell, Storr apparently concentrated on small-scale serving pieces such as this compote. Few other examples in his oeuvre combine cut glass (usually from Bristol factories) with silver.[2] This unusual compote, both decorative and serviceable, embodies the delight the silversmith took in creating small, richly conceived items after he was no longer preoccupied by the large Rundell, Bridge & Rundell commissions.

Form

Similar in design to the butter dish or cooler of the early nineteenth century,[1] this covered compote suggests its intended contents with the grapevine decoration that holds the cut-glass container. A compote—grapes or other fruit preserved in syrup—formed part of the dessert course or augmented other courses as a garnish. This piece, like others of its construction, could have also served as a small container for ice at table.

Engraved Crest

On a wreath, a demi-lion rampant erased collared and holding a fleur-de-lis in the dexter paw.

Unidentified.

1. Clayton, p. 34, pl. 6.
2. See Penzer, 1954, p. 216, pl. LXIX—set of four glass jars with silver mounts and stands.

Benjamin Smith II   English, 1764–after 1818

Born, son of Benjamin Smith I—15 December 1764
Introduced to Matthew Boulton of Birmingham—1790
Partner of Boulton and Smith (with his brother, James Smith III), Birmingham—1792
Benjamin's third son christened "Digby," presumably with Digby Scott as his godparent, suggesting that Smith and Scott were acquainted by this date—1797
Withdrew from Boulton and Smith—1802
First mark entered (Sterling Standard), with Digby Scott as partner, Limekiln Lane, Greenwich—4 October 1802
Second mark entered (Silver Standard, two sizes), with Digby Scott as partner, same address— 21 March 1803
Partnership with Digby Scott dissolved; third mark entered (Sterling Standard), by Smith alone, same address— 11 May 1807
Fourth mark entered (Sterling Standard), by Smith alone, same address—25 June 1807
Fifth mark entered (Sterling Standard), with his brother, James, same address—23 February 1809
Sixth mark entered (Sterling Standard), by Smith alone, same address—14 October 1812
Seventh mark entered (Sterling Standard), by Smith alone, same address—15 January 1814
Eighth mark entered (Sterling Standard), with son, Benjamin III, at Camberwell—5 July 1816
Ninth mark entered (Sterling Standard), same address—25 June 1818
Date of death unrecorded

Digby Scott   English, dates unknown

No record of his apprenticeship through the Goldsmiths' Company nor of his becoming a Freeman of the Company.
First mark entered (Sterling Standard), with Benjamin Smith II as partner, Limekiln Lane, Greenwich—4 October 1802
Second mark entered (Sterling Standard, two sizes), with Benjamin Smith II, same address—21 March 1803
Partnership with Benjamin Smith II dissolved— 11 May 1807

35.   Salver or Tray, 1805

Silver gilt
Extreme height: 3½ in. (8.9 cm.)
Extreme length: 31 in. (78.7 cm.)
Extreme width: 21¼ in. (54 cm.)
Total weight: 230 oz., 12 dwt. (7,172.297 grams)
m. 75.135.46

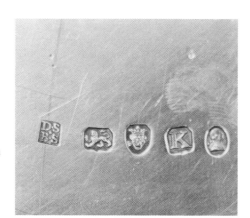

Hallmarks

Digby Scott's and Benjamin Smith's second mark.

Lion passant gardant (Sterling Standard).

Crowned leopard head (London assay).

Capital *K* (letter date for 1805).

Monarch's head (George III) (duty stamp).

Struck under bottom near handle.

Maker's mark, lion passant gardant, and monarch's head struck on bottom of outer cast rim.

Form

See cat. no. 24.

Engraved Arms

The arms and supporters of Lyon, Earl of Beauchamp, with coronet and motto.

Argent two lions passant Gules (Lyon).

A swan Argent wings addorsed Gules, beak and legs Sable, collared and lined Or.

Pendant from the collar of each a shield Gules a fess between six martlets Or (Beauchamp).

The shield ensigned by an earl's coronet.

Supporters: a bear Proper collared muzzled and chained Or.

Motto: *Ex fide fortis* ("Strong through faith").

For William Lyon (1747–1816), descendant in the female line from Richard Lord Beauchamp of Powyke (d. ca. 1496). Lyon was first created Baron Beauchamp of Powyke on 23 February 1806 and later Earl of Beauchamp, 1 December 1815.

From the style of the engraving on the center of this salver and the date of the creation of the Earl of Beauchamp, it is certain that the engraved arms were added sometime after 1 December 1815, at least ten years after the piece was manufactured. Similar, but smaller, salvers or trays[1] made at the same time as this one still exist, suggesting that these salvers might have been part of a larger service.

The unusual construction of the leaf and grape border made this design particularly suited to variations in size. The supporting structure was created from wire as needed, then the cast elements were attached to complete the design. In 1818 Storr used apparently identical molds for a border on a tray,[2] combined with different handles and cast outer rim. Though it is not known exactly how the commissions from Rundell, Bridge & Rundell were divided between Storr and Smith, the same mold makers evidently supplied both.

The feet of this tray are surprising and delightful creations. The elements—animal hooves, human masks, and bold, flanking volutes with honeysuckle fillets—appeared in other silver pieces of this period, but not in these forms. Seemingly unique in Benjamin Smith's productions, these feet are composed of young Bacchus masks with grapevines in their hair and deeply bent hind legs. The position of the Bacchus masks between bent legs gives the appearance of a good-humored crouching faun.

1. There are salvers from the Dodge collection that bear the royal arms, also added after manufacture, and measure only 26 inches in length (*Christie's Review of the Year 1970–71* p. 204, repr.). One from another pair is illustrated in Clayton, pp. 326–27, pl. 46, with later engraving.

2. Penzer, 1954, p. 202, pl. LXII.

36. Pair of Four-Light Candelabra, 1806

(Nozzle inserts, 1809)
Silver gilt
Height: 34¾ in. (88.2 cm.)
Extreme width: 20 in. (50.8 cm.)
Extreme width of bases: 12 in. (30.5 cm.)
Total weight: 865 oz., 16 dwt.
(26,307.872 grams)
1: 442 oz., 14 dwt. (13,146.849 grams)
2: 423 oz., 2 dwt. (13,161.023 grams)
m. 75.135.50a–j

Engraved Crests

On a wreath, a cubit arm in armour grasping a sword Proper.

An earl's coronet above.

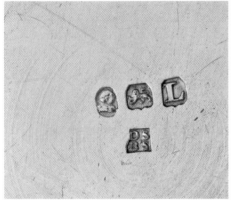

Engraved Inscription

Rundell, Bridge et Rundell aurifices Regis et Principis Wallae Londini fecerunt.

Hallmarks

Benjamin and James Smith's second mark.

Lion passant gardant (Sterling Standard).

Capital *L* (letter date for 1806).

Monarch's head (George III) (duty stamp).

Struck on large nozzles, under side of arm at joint with stem, under sub-base, and under base.

Maker's mark and lion passant gardant struck on underside of wax pan at screw joint.

Maker's mark, lion passant gardant, monarch's head, and letter date *O* for 1809 struck on nozzle inserts.

Applied Arms

Achievement for William Harry, Vane Earl of Darlington (1766–1842), later Marquis of Cleveland (1827) and Duke of Cleveland (1833).

Azure three gauntlets Or.

An earl's coronet above.

Supporters: a griffon Argent collared of the arms and antelope (?) Or collared with a crown charged with three millets (variant for Bolton hind Proper).

Motto: *Nec temere nec timide* ("Neither rashly nor timidly").

Form

See cat. nos. 30 and 32. The Regency period fostered many extravagances. In the first decade of the nineteenth century, even before George, Prince of Wales, was made Regent, his taste for the exotic influenced styles in silver as it did in other media. In those first few years of the new century a desire for exotic variations on prevailing neoclassical designs led to the introduction of Egyptian motifs (see cat. no. 23). These strange decorative fantasies were frequently adapted to large-scale silver, such as these candelabra, as recommended by the architect Charles Heathcote Tatham in his *Designs for Ornamental Plate,* published in 1806.[1]

Benjamin Smith II and James Smith III

1. Oman, 1934, p. 98.
2. Penzer, 1954, p. 172, pl. XLVII, and a similar pair in the Biddle Collection at the White House, Washington, D.C.

Certainly the heaviest and the largest candelabra in the Gilbert Collection, this pair illustrates a style produced by both Storr and the Smiths. Similar branches and bound Egyptianate caryatid stems appear in other pairs by these silversmiths,[2] but here the central shafts are thicker and more massive. The double bases are also heavier than other examples and establish this pair as the most boldly exotic version of this shared design. Liberally mixed with the Egyptian motifs are the familiar neoclassical anthemia, acanthus leaves, and lion masks and paws.

James Smith III   English, dates unknown

Silver gilt
Height: 3⅜ in. (8.6 cm.)
Diameter at rim: 12 in. (30.5 cm.)
Diameter of foot: 5¾ in. (14.6 cm.)
Total weight: 119 oz., 12 dwt.
(3,720.807 grams)
1: 59 oz. (1,835.598 grams)
2: 60 oz., 12 dwt. (1,885.209 grams)
m. 77.2.17a,b

No record of his apprenticeship through the
   Goldsmiths' Company nor of his becoming a
   Freeman of the Company.
Partner of Boulton and Smith (with his brother,
   Benjamin Smith II), Birmingham—1792
Benjamin left Boulton and Smith; James con-
   tinued in Birmingham—1802
Only mark entered (Sterling Standard, three
   sizes), with Benjamin Smith II, Limekiln Lane,
   Greenwich—23 February 1809
Partnership dissolved—by 14 October 1812

Engraved Arms

Azure three crossbows Argent (Sacheville).

Impaling Gules a fess Vair between three unicorns
Argent (Wilkinson).

On a wreath, a stag lodged regardant (unidentified
crest).

All upon a mantle Ermine (this mantle is a sole-
cism for one below the rank of a peer).

Arms are unidentified—no records appear for this
marriage.

Form

   See cat. no. 16. With the neoclassical vogue
of the early nineteenth century, many earlier forms
were revived, resulting in an eclecticism that ma-
tured as the Victorian style. These particular salvers are derived from seventeenth-century English
antecedents.

Hallmarks

Benjamin and James Smith's first mark.

Lion passant gardant (Sterling Standard).

Crowned leopard head (London assay).

1: Capital N (letter date for 1808).

2: Capital P (letter date for 1810).

Monarch's head (George III) (duty stamp).

Struck on outside of foot ring.

1.   Penzer, 1954, p. 176, pl. XLIX.
2.   A similar pair of salvers with different engraving—a
     continuous neoclassical meander with rosettes—by Ben-
     jamin Smith for Rundell, Bridge & Rundell, dated 1807,
     is illustrated in *Art at Auction 1973–74*, p. 285.
3.   Penzer, 1954, p. 176, pl. XLIX.

These footed salvers are particularly interesting examples of the Rundell, Bridge & Rundell style as executed by their major silversmiths, Paul Storr and Benjamin and James Smith. Another pair by the Smiths, identical to this but engraved with the royal arms, is in the collection at Apsley House, London. Penzer illustrates one of a similar pair by Storr, dated 1814, from the collection of Lord Fairhaven.[1] All of these examples share the same construction: a flat circular surface, raised on a trumpet foot, with a cast rim and an engraved pattern of acanthus meanders quartered by fruit baskets.[2] The rims are constructed from cast elements (like those of the large oval tray, cat. no. 35): grape clusters and leaves applied over wire stems and tendrils held within the outer reeded lip ring.

Penzer identifies these salvers as standing fruit dishes,[3] and the grape border and engraved fruit baskets would support this designation.

Silver gilt
Extreme height: 14½ in. (36.8 cm.)
Diameter of stands: 14 in. (35.6 cm.)
Height of coolers: 11¾ in. (29.8 cm.)
Diameter of lip of coolers: 10 in. (25.4 cm.)
Diameter of base of coolers: 5⅛ in. (13 cm.)
Height of stands: 3 in. (7.6 cm.)
Total weight: 504 oz., 1 dwt.
(15,676.998 grams)
1. Cooler and stand: 250 oz., 4 dwt.
(7,781.801 grams)
2. Cooler and stand: 253 oz., 17 dwt.
(7,895.197 grams)
m. 77.2.18a–h

Form

When families started dining unattended in the late eighteenth century the single-bottle wine cooler practically replaced the wine cistern. The earliest known single cooler, in the collection of the Duke of Devonshire, Chatsworth, is by David Willaume and dates from 1698. An equally early (though unmarked) pair of gold coolers was presented to John, first Duke of Marlborough. By the end of the eighteenth century, wine coolers in pairs and sets placed on the table had supplanted the large cistern (see cat. no. 20) placed on the floor or sideboard. During the first half of the nineteenth century the popular vase or urn-shaped cooler (sometimes called an ice bucket) grew taller, raised on a slender stemmed base. With their high centers of gravity, these coolers required broad stands to eliminate the danger of their toppling over and to provide greater ease in carrying the cold metal coolers made damp by condensation.

Hallmarks

Benjamin and James Smith's first mark.

Lion passant gardant (Sterling Standard).

Crowned leopard head (London assay).

Capital *Q* (letter date for 1811).

Monarch's head (George III) (duty stamp).

Struck both inside base ring of coolers and center bottom of stands.

Maker's mark, lion passant gardant, and monarch's head struck on spacer rings.

Maker's mark, lion passant gardant, monarch's head, and letter date *Q* struck on canister.

Maker's mark, lion passant gardant, and letter date *Q* struck on inner edge of top ring with applied grape and leaf relief. Maker's mark, lion passant gardant, and monarch's head stamped on the applied grape and leaf relief on the top ring; on the applied masks on the stands; and on the grape and leaf relief on the stands.

Engraved Arms

Quarterly Crawford, Abernethy, Barclay, and Lindsay with crest, supporters, and motto of Lindsay, Earl of Crawford and Balcarres.

Quarterly 1, Gules a fess Ermine (Crawford).

2, Or a lion Gules over all a bend Sable (Abernethy).

3, Azure a chevron between three crosses formy Or (engraved variant, Argent) (Barclay).

4, Gules a fess checky Argent and Azure (Lindsay).

On a wreath, an ostrich Proper in the beak a key Or (crest of Lindsay, Earl of Crawford and Balcarres).

Supporters: two lions sejant (variant—recorded as gardant and Gules).

Motto: *Endure furth* ("Endure further").

These Scottish arms were not recorded in this form by the Lyon Court, Edinburgh. Since the use of supporters in Scotland is not exclusive to peers of the realm, the coronet, here omitted, is essential for the full achievement.

These crater-shaped wine coolers are fine examples of the Smiths' restrained neoclassicism, with a pleasing balance between bold, crusty decoration and broad expanses of polished silver-gilt surface. Their design is based on a pen drawing (now in the Victoria and Albert Museum)[1] attributed to William Theed (1764–1817), who was a partner and chief modeler of Rundell, Bridge & Rundell. His drawing emphasizes a large relief around the body of the coolers that depicts a triumphal procession of Bacchus, satyrs, nymphs, and attendants in chariots drawn by horses and leopards. Benjamin Smith executed the first set of eight coolers copied exactly from this design in 1808, but it appears that the design then fell to Paul Storr (through some machinations on the part of Rundell, Bridge & Rundell), for all examples with the large relief dated from 1809 on are by that silversmith. However, the coolers seen here prove that the Smiths later produced a simpler version of the Theed design, with a base of their own design. Other decorative elements on these coolers did come from the Theed drawing: the stop-fluting and gadroon-collared stems; the acanthus leaf and blossom relief around the base of the crater itself; the vine and Bacchus-mask handles with spreading grape and tendril motifs; the grapevine meander below the wide rims decorated with a bold egg-and-dart border.

1. Charles Oman, "A Problem of Artistic Responsibility," *Apollo,* March 1966, p. 178, ill. 8.

Benjamin Smith III English, 1793–1850

Silver gilt
Height: 11⅝ in. (29.5 cm.)
Diameter of hip: 7 in. (17.8 cm.)
Diameter of base: 4⅞ in. (12.3 cm.)
Total weight: 38 oz., 19 dwt.
(1,211.92 grams)
m. 75.135.44

Born at 12 Hockley Row near Birmingham—
  6 October 1793
Apprenticed to his father, Benjamin II—
  6 July 1808
Freed from apprenticeship—3 January 1821
First mark entered (Sterling Standard), in
  partnership with his father, at Camberwell—
  5 July 1816
Second mark entered (Sterling Standard),
  alone—15 July 1818
Third mark entered (Sterling Standard), 12 Duke
  Street, Lincoln's Inn Field—24 July 1822
Fourth mark entered (Sterling Standard)—
  1 December 1837

Hallmarks

Benjamin Smith III's fifth mark.

Lion passant (Sterling Standard).

Leopard head (London assay).

Lower-case *t* (letter date for 1834).

Monarch's head (George IV) (duty stamp).

Struck on base.

Maker's mark, lion passant, and leopard head also
struck on handle (inside bottom washer).

Maker's mark, lion passant, and letter date struck
inside lid.

Form

In the eighteenth century, jugs were used to
serve many beverages, such as water, coffee, ale,
and claret. The popularity of this vessel received
new impetus in the 1830s with the widespread
fondness for mulled claret (a vogue enthusiastically
supported by George IV). Generally, jugs destined
to serve the fashionable hot wine were distinguished by decorative grape motifs and by ivory
rings that kept the handle a comfortable temperature. The popularity of claret coincided with the
introduction of frosted glass, and frequently claret
jugs of this period have frosted glass bodies
mounted with silver necks, lids, and handles.

This vase-shaped jug, though produced during the brief reign of William IV, retains elements of
early nineteenth-century neoclassicism in the chased fluting and acanthus foliage adorning the circular
foot, base of the jug, shoulder, and lip. The bold execution of these elements reflects the training that
Benjamin Smith III received from his father and demonstrates his abilities in casting and chasing vividly
elegant forms.

The high curved handle, cast in three parts separated by ivory insulation rings, represents cattails
and leaves. No grapes or other motifs indicate a specific function for the jug, although the ivory rings
make certain that it was intended for hot liquids. The pale lemony gilding, now well worn, bears witness
to the use the piece has received.

If any element of this jug suggests an incipient Victorianism, it is the unusual scenes of horse racing
and riding. Indicating the possibility that this jug was created as a presentation trophy, these deeply
engraved scenes on arbitrarily placed mat panels bespeak a decorative technique that was to be popular in
the later decades of the century.

40.   Set of Four Candlesticks, 1821

(Detachable wax pans, 1825)
Extreme height: 13½ in. (34.3 cm.)
Extreme width of bases: 7½ in. (19 cm.)
Height of sticks without pans: 12½ in. (31.7 cm.)
Total weight: 189 oz., 2 dwt.
(5,882.418 grams)
1: 47 oz., 12 dwt. (1,481.235 grams)
2: 48 oz., 15 dwt. (1,516.672 grams)
3: 46 oz., 19 dwt. (1,459.974 grams)
4: 45 oz., 16 dwt. (1,424.537 grams)
m. 77.2.19a–h

No record of his apprenticeship through the
Goldsmiths' Company nor of his becoming a
Freeman of the Company. Known for produc-
tion of unusual Regency plate, generally in
rococo revival style.
First mark entered (Sterling Standard), 18 King's
Head Court, Holborn Hill—27 April 1813
Second mark entered (Sterling Standard), same
address—20 May 1813
Moved to 24 Bridge Street, Covent Gardens—
26 September 1818
Third mark entered (Sterling Standard, two sizes),
same address—17 March 1819

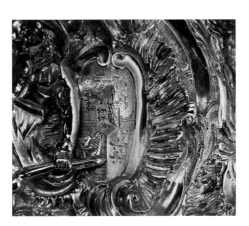

Engraved Arms

Quarterly England, Scotland, and Ireland with
Hanover in pretense, a label (uncharged) for one of
the sons of George III as used after 1801 and before 1837. The absence of the charges on the label
and the motto make further identification impossible. The arms are definitely not those of George
IV (nor those for him as Prince Regent, 1812–20).

Arthur Grimwade suggests that these sticks were
commissioned before George III died in January
1820 and executed before the coronation of George
IV in July 1821, and that the engraver was thus
correct in recording these arms for George IV.

Form

Since sculptural figurative sticks have always
proven both difficult and expensive to produce,
they have generally appeared only in periods of
economic stability and opulence. They were popular briefly in the late seventeenth century and
again in the 1770s.

With the taste for exoticism that flourished
during the Regency, these picturesque creations
were produced in considerable numbers, and by
Victoria's reign, near mid-century, sculptural
candlesticks and candelabra with groups of figures
were again in vogue.

Hallmarks

Edward Farrell's third mark.

Lion passant gardant (Sterling Standard).

Crowned leopard head (London assay).

Lower-case *f* (letter date for 1821).

Monarch's head (George III) (duty stamp).[1]

Struck on top surface of triangular bases.

Nozzles struck as above, but with lower-case *k*
(letter date for 1825).

These exotic candlesticks are the odd creations of an age of curiosities. Reactions against the formality of neoclassicism, they herald the later Victorian taste, when surface complexity was to replace balanced composition.

Combining the established baluster form with high-relief figures, these composite sticks present a less than unified appearance. The pyramidal bases are assembled from three elaborately cast triangles encrusted with deep waves, foliage, and a rococo shell cartouche containing the curiously engraved royal arms. Over the soldered joints of these bases lounge male figures in seventeenth-century peasant costumes with wide-brimmed hats, eating, drinking, and playing violins.

The stems that rise from a cast nob at the apex of each base were created in three separate castings and their joints are still visible through the indifferent chasing: at the ring below the "Chinaman's" feet; immediately above his hat on all four sides of the square cornucopialike stem he holds; and, less visible, at the slender turned necks of the sockets. This casual approach to the final chasing of joints would never have been tolerated in the eighteenth century, but it became more acceptable in the industrialized nineteenth century.

The prancing, exotically costumed "Chinamen" on the stems have given rise (on the strength of their costumes and the curious engraved arms) to the suggestion that these candlesticks were intended for use at the Brighton Pavilion. No document, however, substantiates this suggestion.

George, Prince Regent, was not unfamiliar with the Chinese style when these were made. He had, in fact, furnished a Chinese drawing room[2] at his ill-fated Carlton House before the turn of the century. Under his supervision, the Brighton Pavilion underwent numerous redecorations between 1802 and 1815, with the assistance of Crace & Sons, the prince's "decorators." A more sophisticated Chinese style was evident in the interiors from 1815 to 1818, when the Pavilion was all but completed. After George III's death in January 1820, both the soon to be crowned George IV and his decorators were too busy with preparations for the coronation to order any additions for Brighton—and would certainly not have accepted the unsophisticated examples seen here. These "exotics" were probably commissioned by one of George IV's six brothers. Perhaps Farrell's royal patron was the same one who ordered the pilgrim bottles (see cat. no. 41) that bear the arms of the Duke of York, who in the 1820s squandered a fortune on spectacular building.

1. The George III mark struck here is an erroneous carryover of the dead monarch's stamp.
2. Illustrated in Thomas Sheraton, *Appendix to Furniture Makers' and Upholsterers' Drawing-Book,* 1791–94, reprint ed., New York, 1970, pp. 50–51, pls. 31, 32.

41.   **Pair of Pilgrim Bottles,** 1825

Silver gilt
Height: 17 in. (43.2 cm.)
Extreme width: 10¼ in. (25.8 cm.)
Diameter of base: 5¼ in. (13.5 cm.)
Total weight: 350 oz., 8 dwt.
(7,888.788 grams)
1:   122 oz., 12 dwt. (3,812.941 grams)
2:   127 oz., 16 dwt. (3,975.947 grams)
m. 77.2.20a–d

Hallmarks

Edward Farrell's third mark.

Lion passant (Sterling Standard).

Leopard head (London assay).

Lower-case *k* (letter date for 1825).

Monarch's head (George IV) (duty stamp).

Struck on necks.

Maker's mark, lion passant, and letter date struck
on applied outer leaves of lid.

Lion passant and letter date struck inside lid.

Engraved Arms

The arms of the Duke of York.

Quarterly 1 and 4, Gules three lions passant
gardant Or (England).

2, Or a lion rampant within a double tressure
flory-counterflory Gules (Scotland).

3, Azure a harp Or stringed Argent (Ireland).

Royal arms with inescutcheon and differenced by a
label of three points Argent.

Within a Garter.

A helm and ducal coronet above.

Supporters: Dexter, a lion gardant crowned and
labeled; Sinister, a unicorn Argent labeled armed
and chained Or.

Motto: *Quo pax et gloria ducunt* ("Led by peace and
glory").

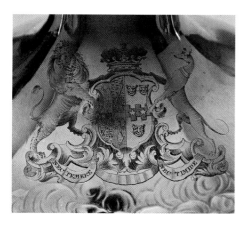

Engraved Arms

For William Harry, Vane Earl of Darlington (1766–1842), later Marquis of Cleveland (1827) and Duke of Cleveland (1833).

Quarterly 1 and 4, Azure three dexter gauntlets Or (Vane).

2 and 3, quarterly 1 and 4, quarterly France and England.

2, Scotland.

3, Ireland.

Over all a baton couped sinister (Ermine, but the spots have been omitted) (Fitzroy).

Impaling Argent (variant for Or) a fess counter-embattled Sable between three leopard faces Azure two molets Argent (Russell).

A marquis's coronet above.

Supporters: a lion gardant crowned Or collared gobony Ermine and Azure and a greyhound Argent collared Ermine and Azure.

Motto: *Nec temere nec timide* ("Neither rashly nor timidly").

continued

Engraved Crests

On a ducal coronet, a crowned lion statant gardant Or (crest of the Duke of York). All within the Garter and ensigned by a ducal coronet.

Engraved Inscription

Lewis Silversmiths to H. R. H. the Duke of York, St. James's, London.

Struck on edge of foot, partially obliterated, with an original inscription barely visible beneath.

Form

These silver bottles received their names and shapes from the early leather flagons carried by pilgrims and crusaders. The flattened pear shape, adapted from rounded flagons or livery pots, permitted the traveler to wear the flask suspended from his hip by a chain. The original source also inspired the chained lid, which enabled the flask to be used while riding without the risk of losing the stopper. The few early silver pilgrim bottles that survived from the seventeenth century were usually retained as sideboard plate.

With the revival of this form by Huguenot silversmiths in the eighteenth century, new, more impressive examples were created for the sideboard, some measuring over thirty inches in height.[1] Some nineteenth-century versions incorporate religious scenes as part of their decoration, reflecting their religious associations.

1. Clayton, p. 199.

The Huguenot influence is evident here in the lambrequinlike decorations applied at the bottom of the flattened ovals and in the grotesque masks that serve as mounts for the fine carrying chains.

Repoussé biblical scenes fill one side of each flagon (one represents Christ in the temple, the other, Christ's Ascension) and are probably based on eighteenth-century engravings. The reverse sides display the engraved arms of the Duke of York. At the base of the necks above the repoussé scenes are engraved the arms of the Marquis of Cleveland, who purchased these pilgrim bottles at the sale of the Duke of York's plate in 1827 and added his arms to their already illustrious heraldry.

Robert Garrard I English, 1758–1818

Height: 1⅜ in. (3.5 cm.)
Diameter: 9½ in. (24.1 cm.)
Total weight: 57 oz., 5 dwt.
(1,780.672 grams)
1: 28 oz., 12 dwt. (889.45 grams)
2: 28 oz., 13 dwt. (891.222 grams)
m. 75.135.45a,b

Apprenticed to Stephen Unwin of the Grocers'
Co., hardware man, Cheapside, London, for
initial training as metal worker in other than
precious metals—7 October 1773
Freed from apprenticeship, mentioned as em-
ployed "at Messrs. Wakelin & Co. Goldsmith,
Panton Street, Haymarket, London"—
2 November 1780
First mark entered (Sterling Standard), with John
Wakelin as partner, Panton Street, Haymarket,
London—20 October 1792
Second mark entered (Sterling Standard), alone,
same address—11 August 1802

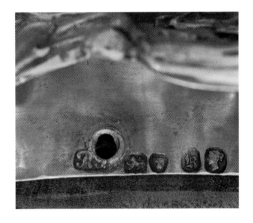

Hallmarks

Robert Garrard's third mark.

Lion passant (Sterling Standard).

Leopard head (London assay).

Lower-case *k* (letter date for 1845).

Monarch's head (Victoria) (duty stamp).

Struck on outer bottom of rim (maker's mark
pierced with silver screw).

Form

Alternately known as bottle stands, decanter
stands, wine slides, and wine coasters, these low,
circular stands were one of several new silver forms
popularized about 1760. With the new custom of
dismissing servants from the room in favor of private dining there evolved the gentlemen-only
period after dinner for drinking, smoking, and
uninhibited conversation. When helping oneself
to wine from a bottle or decanter, inevitably more
drips resulted than when one was served by the
well-trained hand of a skilled domestic. As a result, coasters such as these were provided in sets of
two, four, six, or eight to protect the table linen.

Cast and Chased Arms

The achievement of Rothschild as Baron of the
Austrian Empire, 29 September 1822.

Quarterly 1, Or an eagle displaying Sable.

2 and 3, Azure an arm issuing from the flank
proper grasping five arrows, points downward
Argent.

4, Or a lion rampant Gules.

A scocheon Gules an oval buckler in bend sinister
Argent.

Three crests, each on a barred helmet: Dexter, out
of a crown Or, two proboscides Or and Sable supporting a molet of six points Or.

Center, out of a crown an eagle displayed (no
tincture recorded).

Sinister, out of a crown three ostrich feathers
Azure, Argent, and Azure.

Supporters: a lion Or and a unicorn Argent.

Motto: *Concordia Integritas Industria* ("Harmony,
Integrity, Industry").

For Lionel Nathan Rothschild (1808–1879). The
Rothschild family, first ennobled in 1817, were
created Barons of the Austrian Empire, 29 September 1822. Lionel Nathan Rothschild had royal
license to use the Austrian title and arms in England in 1838. After several elections to Parliament by the City of London, Baron Lionel Nathan
Rothschild was finally permitted by an act of Parliament in 1858 to become the first member of the
Jewish faith to take a seat in the Commons.[1]

1. Dodds, p. 312.

The only pieces of truly Victorian silver in the Gilbert Collection, these wine coasters demonstrate what that era did to the rococo style in revival. Compared to examples by de Lamerie in the truly rococo spirit, these coasters exemplify the thickening of detail and complexity of decoration that was essential to Victorian surface embellishment.

Created in two parts—flat centers and deeply cast rings—these pieces are held to their wooden backing by silver screws (possibly not original, since they pierce the maker's marks). The flat centers have been given entirely to the presentation of the heraldic arms. The deep rings are cast in meanders of thick seaweedlike scrolls that define ten panels, each decorated with cast mythological creatures relating to the sea and water: Neptune, Amphitrite, naiads, paired demi-seahorses, dolphins, etc.

Though the Garrard ledgers for this period still exist, they bear no record of these coasters having been directly commissioned by the Baron Rothschild. This may indicate that an agent of the baron placed the order in his own name or, more likely, that the coasters were created with blank centers for stock and the baron's arms were later added.

Gregory Chizhevski

Kiev, Ukraine, active last decades of
the eighteenth century

Cyrillic Inscription

These Gates in the Church of the Nativity of the
Mother of God were made during the reign of the
very Orthodox Sovereign Empress Ekaterina
Alexeievna and her Heir the Orthodox Sovereign
Tsesarevich, Grand Duke Pavel Petrovich, and his
spouse the Orthodox Lady Grand Duchess Maria
Fedorovna and the Orthodox Lords and Grand
Dukes Alexander Pavlovich and Konstantin Pav-
lovich and the Orthodox Lady the Grand Duchess
Alexandra Pavlovna, with the blessings of the Lord
Archimandrite Father Zosim Valkevich of the
Kievo Pecherskaia Lavra, and with the dedicated
devotion of the Keeper of the same Pechera the
Elder of the Church Brother Vitali. The year
1784, 31st day of March. The weight in silver is 2
pouds, 6 lots [1,087 troy oz.—33,820.357
grams]. Thirty-five foreign chervonets [ducats]
were used for gilding.

The Gilbert's two pairs of Royal Gates were originally part of two separate churches in the
Monastery of Pechersk in Kiev.[1] Founded in the mid-eleventh century, the monastery stretches over
sixty-nine wooded acres on the right bank of the Dnieper River. The Upper Monastery and the Far Caves
are on two hills; in a hollow between them are the Near Caves. Throughout numerous invasions, the
monastery sustained a high level of religious and cultural activity, supporting workshops that provided
the rich religious community with expert woodcarvers, builders, silversmiths, printers, engravers, etc.
These Royal Gates are the product of such a workshop.

The Church of the Nativity of the Mother of God, from which this pair of gates came, was built in
1696, and stands on the hilly territory of the Far Caves. Master Gregory Chizhevski received a commission from the fathers of the monastery to make "for the Church of the Nativity of the Kievo-Pecherskaia
Lavra Royal Gates of silver and silver gilt."[2] No hallmarks are known for Chizhevski.

Traditionally Royal Gates show five scenes: the Annunciation in the upper row, the four Evangelists
below. The Gilbert gates differ only slightly from this prescribed iconographical pattern: there are six
icons in bas-relief, framed in an ornamental cartouche and placed symmetrically on both leaves of the
gates. On the left is the Annunciation; below, St. Matthew, with pen, book, and angel; and still lower,
St. Mark, with pen, book, and lion. On the right appears the Entry into Jerusalem, surmounting two
icons, one below the other, that represent St. John, with pen, book, and eagle, and St. Luke, with his ox.

In the visual center of the Royal Gates, on the vertical projecting molding, a small engraved oval
icon depicts Christ-Pantocrator, with one hand blessing and the other holding the Gospel. Above the
inscription at the bottom of each gate is a basket of flowers and leaves enclosed in a medallion, which
adds a decorative touch to the composition.

The lavish elegance of these monumental gates is enhanced by interlaced garlands of flowers and
foliage that are cast, chiseled, and chased in sculptured deep relief to create a dramatic play of light and
dark. The use of rocaille-inspired scrolls, curves, and counter-curves adds grace to the design. The
pierced work lightens the entire surface and modifies the luxurious massivenesss of the "Ukrainian
Baroque," the prevailing style of the time. With his striking combination of old native carving traditions
with newly acquired motifs and patterns, Master Chizhevski created one of the most exceptional Royal
Gates of his era.

43. Royal Gates, 1784

Church of the Nativity of the Mother of God
Silver and silver gilt
Height: 91½ in. (235 cm.)
Width: 40½ in. (103 cm.)
m. 77.1.8a,b

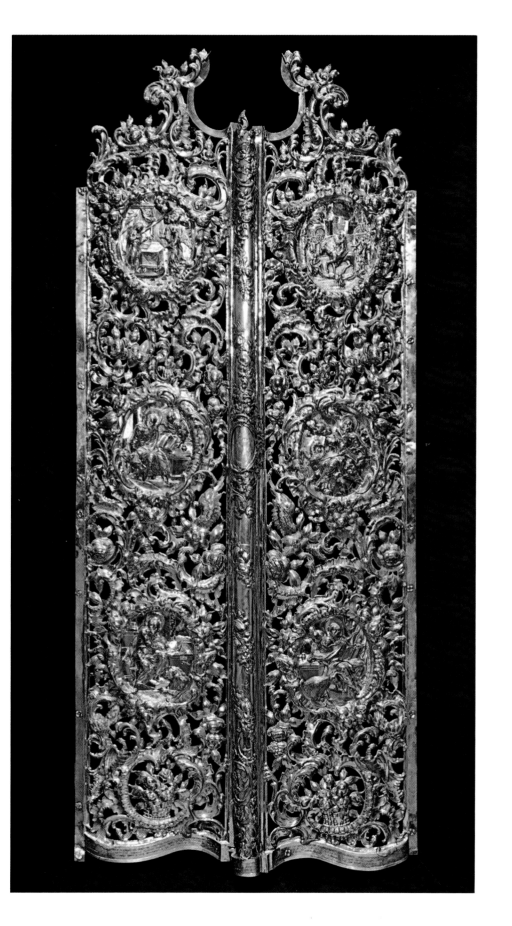

Form

Royal Gates, or Holy Gates, are the dramatic
focal point of an *iconostasis*. A continuous wall-like
screen to conceal the altar at the eastern end of a
church, the *iconostasis* is formed by rows of individual icons mounted vertically in prescribed
iconographical patterns. The prototype of the
iconostasis goes back to the time of Emperor Justi-
nian (527–565). Always double doors, the Royal
Gates are the largest of three openings in an *iconostasis* and the most important architectural element
in the interior of an Eastern Orthodox church.
They not only isolate the congregation from the
Sanctuary where the sacrament of Eucharist is cel-
ebrated, but have a specific liturgical function and
symbolize the entrance into the kingdom of God.
While usually closed, the Royal Gates are opened
at certain moments during the service when the
Holy Eucharist is brought forward by the priest.

1. When the government of the U.S.S.R. secularized and
    nationalized monasteries many ecclesiastical objects were
    sold to foreign collectors.
2. Documented in the State Central Historical Archives,
    Kiev, U.S.S.R.

Alexis Timothy Ishchenko Kiev, Ukraine (died in 1811)   44. Royal Gates, 1784

Church of the Elevation of the Holy Cross
Silver gilt
Height: 106 in. (269.2 cm.)
Width: 49½ in. (125.1 cm.)
m. 77.2.21a,b

Hallmark

AH 12

The stone structure of the Church of the Elevation of the Holy Cross, built in 1700 in the Near Caves, dates from the period of revived architectural activity in Kiev that followed the War of Liberation (1648–54). At this time great emphasis was placed on the decoration of church interiors, especially of the *iconostasis,* which during the seventeenth and eighteenth centuries became a complex three-dimensional background for icons. These Royal Gates formed part of such a decoration, and the richly carved and gilded *iconostasis* for which they were created in 1784 is still part of the church interior. They were made by Alexis Timothy Ishchenko, who produced numerous other ecclesiastical objects. According to documents in the State Central Historical Archives in Kiev, he made in "1784 for the Church of the Elevation in the Near Caves, Royal Gates of gilded silver." His mark was *AИ* which appears as *AH* on the object. The hallmark *12* specifies that the silver content falls approximately between 34% and 57%.

The iconography of these gates deviates from the traditional subjects. A Crucifixion in the upper center symbolizes the triumph and the glorification of God incarnate. Three main themes—the Incarnation, the Passion, and Christ's divinity—are expressed in the six medallions below, which depict the Annunciation, Christ's Entry into Jerusalem, the Presentation of Christ in the Temple, the Presentation of the Virgin in the Temple, the Transfiguration, and the Raising of Lazarus. Three additional scenes are shown on the central vertical molding. The first small oval medallion has two images: a Deësis, above an angel supporting an elevated cross, a reference to the Church of the Elevation of the Cross. The second medallion presents the Adoration of the Shepherds, a scene recalling the Feast of the Nativity. In the last medallion the Uspenski Cathedral of the Pechersk Monastery is framed by the two founders of the Monastery: St. Anthony and St. Theodosius. Christ's ancestors are represented on the extreme lower field of the gates; on the left, David as king with crown and harp, and on the right, Jesse, father of David.

The elaborate monumental framework of the cast, embossed, and chased Royal Gates belongs to the style called "Kievan" or "Ukrainian" Baroque. The C- and S-scrolls, shells, grooves, and other slender rocaille motifs are arranged in unpredictable asymmetry, producing a rich ornamental complexity. The low-relief work gives the gates a two-dimensional appearance, while the *à jour* treatment of the entire pattern creates an effect of unity and lightness. The tradition of the Ukrainian woodcarver is visible in the workmanship, concept, and execution of this spectacular work of art.

Form

See cat. no. 43.

Cyrillic Inscription

These Gates in the Church of the Elevation of the
Holy Cross were made during the reign of the very
Orthodox Sovereign Empress Ekaterina Alexeievna
and her Heir the Orthodox Sovereign Tsesarevich,
Grand Duke Pavel Petrovich, and his spouse the
Orthodox Lady Grand Duchess Maria Feodorovna
and the Orthodox Lords and Grand Dukes Alexander Pavlovich and Konstantin Pavlovich and
the Orthodox Lady the Grand Duchess Alexandra
Pavlovna, with the blessings of the Lord Archimandrite Father Zosim Valkevich of the Kievo
Pecherskaia Lavra. In the year 1784, ninth day of
the month of June, the weight in silver is 2 pouds,
17 founts, 2 lots [1,293 troy oz.—36,656.55
grams]. Ninety-five foreign chervonets [ducats]
were used for gilding. At the expense of the good-
hearted donors, under [in the presence of] the
Keeper of the Pechera the Elder of the Church
Brother Markian.

Collections and Literature

1. Two-Handled Covered Cup, 1717
Collections: Charles John Halswell, ninth Baron
Wharton (1908–1959), Halswell Park, Somerset,
and Setubal, Portugal; Christie's, London, 1969;
J. H. Bourdon-Smith, Ltd., London.
Literature: *Christie's Review of the Year 1969–70,*
London, 1971, repr. p. 211; Hillier, p. 114, ill. 1
on p. 115.

2. Pair of Two-Light Sconces, ca. 1725
Collections: Thomas Foley, M. P. (d. 1737); the
Barons Foley of Kidderminster; Worshipful
Company of Goldsmiths, London; Madame
Farago; Hon. Mrs. A. M. Holman; Christie's,
London, 15 July 1925, lot no. 80; Florence, Lady
Trent, Jersey; J. A. Mango, Esq.; Partridge
(Fine Arts) Ltd., London.
Literature: Phillips, p. 81, pl. XXXVII; *Art at
Auction, 1966–67,* p. 296, repr. in color on p. 301;
Clayton, p. 248; Hillier, p. 114, ill. 2 on p. 115.

3. Strawberry Dish, 1726
Collections: S. J. Phillips, Ltd., London.

4. Kettle on Stand, 1730
Collections: Richard Ogden, London.
Literature: Hillier, p. 114, ill. 4 on p. 115.

5. Two-Handled Basket, 1731
Collections: Partridge (Fine Arts) Ltd., London.
Literature: Hillier, p. 114, ill. 7 on p. 116.

Pair of Sauceboats on Stands with Ladles

6. Boats, 1733
Collections: Phillip Yorke of Erddig, Denbigshire
(1743–1804); Christie's, London, 13 June 1945,
lot no. 84; S. J. Phillips, Ltd., London; Christie's,
London, 27 November 1957, lot no. 129; Hon.
Violet Vivian, London; Sotheby's, London,
4 June 1974, lot no. 84; Shrubsole, Incorporated,
New York.
Literature: M. A. Q., "English Silver for Collec-
tors," *Apollo,* LIV, December 1951, fig. V, p. 174
(one of pair with ladles); Grimwade, 1974, pl. 32a.

7. Stands, 1739
Collections: Phillip Yorke of Erddig, Denbigshire
(1743–1804); S. J. Phillips, Ltd., London; Hon.
Violet Vivian, London; Sotheby's, London,
4 June 1974, lot no. 84; Shrubsole, Incorporated,
New York.
Literature: M. A. Q., "English Silver for Collec-
tors," *Apollo,* LIV, December 1951, fig. V, p. 174
(one of pair with ladles); Clayton, p. 243, ill. 477b.

8. Ladles, ca. 1740
Collections: Phillip Yorke of Erddig, Denbigshire
(1743–1804); S. J. Phillips, Ltd., London; Hon.
Violet Vivian, London; Sotheby's, London, 4 June
1974, lot no. 71; Shrubsole, Incorporated, New York.
Literature: M. A. Q., "English Silver for Collec-
tors," *Apollo,* LIV, December 1951, fig. V, p. 174
(one of pair with ladles).

9. Kettle on Stand, 1736
Collections: David Orgell, Inc., Beverly Hills.
Literature: Hillier, p. 114, ill. 3 on p. 115.

10. Kettle on Stand with Tray, 1736–37
Collections: John Gibbitas, Esq., Weston Lodge,
Ross-on-Wye, Gloustershire; Sotheby's, London,
27 June 1919; William Randolph Hearst, New
York; Bryan Jenks, Esq.; Christie's, London,
16 June 1965, lot no. 35; Sir George Doughty;
J. H. Bourdon-Smith, Ltd., London.
Literature: Phillips, pp. 100–101, pl. CXIV;
Christie's Review of the Year 1964–65, London,
1966, repr. p. 133; Hillier, p. 114, ills. 5 and 6 on
p. 116.

11. Punch Ladle, 1738
Collections: Phillips Garden, London, sale, 1751;
Christie's, London, 15 April 1931, lot no. 103;
Messrs. Critchton Bros., London; Sotheby's, New
York, 4 June 1974, lot no. 72; Shrubsole, Incorpo-
rated, New York.
Literature: Phillips, p. 103, pls. CXXII, CXXIV;
Art at Auction, 1973–74, repr. p. 284.

12. Pair of Covered Soup Tureens, 1722–42
Collections: The Earls of Mount Edgcumbe,
Plymouth; Shrubsole, Incorporated, New York;
Mr. and Mrs. Arthur D. Leidesdorf, New York;
Sotheby's, London, 4 June 1974; Shrubsole,
Incorporated, New York.

13. Pair of Soup Ladles, 1748
Collections: The Earls of Mount Edgcumbe,
Plymouth; Shrubsole, Incorporated, New York;
Mr. and Mrs. Arthur D. Leidesdorf, New York;
Sotheby's, London, 4 June 1974; Shrubsole,
Incorporated, New York.

14. Pair of Candlesticks, 1741
Collections: Stuart Albert Samuel Montagu, third
Baron Swaythling (1898–1942), Townhill Park,
Southampton; Christie's (?), London, 6 May 1942,
lot no. 15; Eric Shrubsole, Ltd., London.
Literature: Phillips, p. 105, pl. CXXXII
(repr. with nozzles).

15. Basket, 1741
Collections: Judge Irwin Untermeyer; S. J.
Phillips, Ltd., London.

16. Pair of Salvers, 1741
Collections: Algernon Coote, sixth Earl of
Montrath; the Earls of Montrath; Frank Zoringer,
Wilmire, Kentucky; Partridge (Fine Arts) Ltd.,
London; Shrubsole, Incorporated, New York.

17. Ewer and Basin, 1742
Collections: Algernon Coote, sixth Earl of
Montrath; the Earls of Montrath; Earl of
Portarlington (to 1881); Colonel A. Heywood
Lonsdale; Christie's, London, 27 June 1956, lot
no. 126; Sir George Doughty; J. H. Bourdon-
Smith, Ltd., London.
Literature: Edwards and Ramsey, eds., III, pp. 76,
78, pl. 41.; "West County Treasures," *Antique
Collector,* October 1967, pp. 230–33, repr. p. 231;
Clayton, p. 169, ill. 336 (ewer only); Grimwade,
1974, p. 48, ill. 54B (ewer only); Hillier, p. 118,
ill. 8a, b.

18. Two-Handled Covered Cup, 1742
Collections: William Cowper (1709–1764), Earl
Cowper, Viscount Fordwich, and Baron Cowper of
Wingham; Sir Charles Jackson; Christie's, Lon-
don, 24 November 1971, lot no. 33; Viscountess
Gate; Shrubsole, Incorporated, New York.
Literature: Hillier, pp. 114, 118, ill. 9 on p. 119.

19. Basket, ca. 1745
Collections: P. L. Pickles & Co., Sydney,
Australia; S. J. Phillips, Ltd., London.
Literature: Hillier, p. 118, ill. 10a, b on p. 119.

20. Wine Cistern, 1794
Collections: Augustus Frederick (1773–1843),
sixth son of George III, Duke of Sussex, Earl of In-
verness, and Baron of Arklow; Christie's, London,
June/July 1843; the Hussy-Packe family; Christie's, London, 9 July 1947; L. T. Locan, London (?);
Christie's, London, 23 May 1962; Shrubsole,
Incorporated, New York.
Literature: Reitlinger, p. 658; Clayton, p. 338,
ill. 716; *Christie's Review of the Season, 1975*, London, 1975, p. 199, repr.

21. Basket, 1797
Collections: Victor Rothschild, Esq.; Sotheby's,
London, 26 April 1937, lot no. 20, pl. II; Francis
Stonor, London; Sotheby's, London, 15 October
1970, lot no. 79, ill. and color frontispiece; Mrs.
Fay Plohn, New York; Shrubsole, Incorporated,
New York.
Literature: Penzer, 1954, p. 98, pl. X; *Art at
Auction, 1970–71*, repr. pl. 309; Hillier, p. 118,
ill. 11 on p. 120.

22. Tea Urn, 1802
Collections: William Henry Vane, the third Earl
of Darlington; the Vane Earls of Darlington; Baron
Barnard and Marquis of Cleveland, Raby Castle,
Winchelsea, Durham; Christie's, London, 15 July
1975, lot no. 143, ill. and color frontispiece;
Shrubsole, Incorporated, New York, to
18 September 1975.
Literature: Hillier, p. 118, ill. 12 on p. 120.

23. Set of Four Soup Tureens, 1806–7
Collections: Duke of Cumberland; Mrs. Fay
Plohn, New York; Lillian and Morrie A. Moss,
Memphis, Tennessee.
Literature: E. A. Jones, "The Duke of Cumberland's Plate," *National Review,* 1920; *Country Life,*
8 November 1924; Moss, pp. 254–56, pl. 189
(one); *Art at Auction, 1970–71,* p. 300, one repr.
on p. 307; Honour, two repr. in color on p. 226.

24. Salver or Tray, 1808
Collections: John George, fourth Baron Monson
(1785–1809), Bath; the Barons of Monson; Francis Stonor, London; Sotheby's, London, 15 October
1970; S. J. Phillips, Ltd., London.
Literature: Penzer, 1954, p. 128, pl. XXV.

25. Jug on Stand, 1809
Collections: J. H. Bourdon-Smith, Ltd., London.

26. Dessert Stand, 1810
Collections: David Orgell, Inc., Beverly Hills.

27. Centerpiece, 1813
Collections: J. H. Bourdon-Smith, Ltd., London.
Literature: Hillier, p. 119, ill. 14 on p. 121.

28. Warwick Vase, 1814
Collections: The Macgregor family; David Orgell,
Inc., Beverly Hills.

29. Punch Ladle, 1814
Collections: Corporation of Dover, Kent; Lillian
and Morrie A. Moss, Memphis, Tennessee; David
Orgell, Inc., Beverly Hills.
Literature: Jewitt and St. John Hope, pp. 327–
28, repr. p. 325; Knocker, pp. 23–24, repr.;
Penzer, 1954, p. 184, pl. LIII; Clayton, p. 216,
ill. 421; Moss, p. 242, pl. 180.

30. Set of Four Candlesticks, 1815
Collections: Christie's, London, 24 November 1971,
lot no. 45; Shrubsole, Incorporated, New York.
Literature: Penzer, 1954, Appendix A, p. 248.

31. Soy Frame, 1816
Collections: S. J. Phillips, Ltd., London.

32. Pair of Four-Light Candelabra, 1816
Collections: The Barons Foley, Worcester; Christie's, London, 18 June 1924, lot no. 64; Shrubsole, Incorporated, New York.
Literature: Penzer, 1954, Appendix A, p. 249.

33. Pair of Covered Entree Dishes, 1816–17
Collections: Bernard Edward, twelfth Duke of Norfolk (b. 1765); the Dukes of Norfolk; Shrubsole, Incorporated, New York.
Literature: Hillier, p. 121, ill. 15.

34. Covered Compote, 1820
Collections: Marshall Field & Co., Chicago.
Literature: Wyler, p. 15, repr.

35. Salver or Tray, 1805
Collections: Sotheby's, London, 11 February 1971; J. H. Bourdon-Smith, London.

36. Pair of Four-Light Candelabra, 1806
Collections: William Henry Vane, the third Earl of Darlington; the Vane Earls of Darlington; Baron Barnard and Marquis of Cleveland, Raby Castle, Winchelsea, Durham; Christie's, London, 15 July 1975, lot no. 141, repr.
Literature: Frank Davis, "Talking about Sales Rooms," *Country Life,* 9 October 1975, pp. 910–11, fig. 3; *Christie's Review of the Season, 1975,* London, 1975, p. 208, only one repr.

37. Pair of Footed Salvers, 1808, 1810

38. Pair of Wine Coolers on Stands, 1811
Collections: The Earls of Crawford and Balcarres, Haigh Hall, Wigan, Lancashire; Christie's, London, 10 October 1946, lot no. 71; A. B. Gilbert, London; Sir William Butin, M. B. E.; Christie's, London, 20 November 1968, lot no. 57.
Literature: *Christie's Review of the Year, 1968–69,* London, 1969, p. 185, only one of pair repr.

39. Jug, 1834
Collections: Rt. Hon. the Lord Wharton; Christie's, London, 18 March 1970, lot no. 89.

40. Set of Four Candlesticks, 1821
Collections: Christie's, London, 24 November 1971, lot no. 45 (as "property of a gentleman").
Literature: *Christie's Review of the Season, 1972,* London, 1972, p. 198, two of the set repr.

41. Pair of Pilgrim Bottles, 1825
Collections: Frederick, Duke of York (d. 1827) (George III's second son); Duke of York sale, Christie's, London, 1827; Marquis of Cleveland, 1827; Christie's, London, 15 July 1975, lot no. 134, only one repr. on p. 34 and color frontispiece.
Literature: Hillier, p. 121, ill. 13 on p. 120.

42. Pair of Wine Coasters, 1845
Collections: Baron Lionel Nathan Rothschild.

43. Royal Gates, 1784
Collections: W. R. Hearst, 1935–60; S. J. Phillips, Ltd., London, 1962; Francis Stonor, 1962–72; S. J. Phillips, Ltd., London, 1972.
Literature: *Kratkoe Istoricheskoe Opisanie Kievo-Pecherskoi Lavry,* Kiev: Tipografia Akademii Kievskoi, 1805, pp. 39, 45 (in Russian); Evgeni, Metropolitan of Kiev and Galizia, *Opisanie Kievo-Pecherskoi Lavry,* Kiev: Kievo-Pecherskaia Lavra, 1826, pp. 71, 126 (in Russian); E. E. Bolkhovitinov, *Opisanie Kievo-Pecherskoi Lavry,* Kiev: Kievo-Pecherskaia Lavra, 1831, p. 86 (in Russian); "Cathedral Gates in Silver Gilt," *The Antique Collector,* April 1961, pp. 66, 67, repr.; M. Z. Petrenko, *Ukrainske Zolotarstvo XVI–XVIII,* Kiev: Naukova Dumka, 1969, p. 193 (in Ukrainian); Hillier, p. 121, ill. A (color) on p. 117.

44. Royal Gates, 1784
Collections: W. R. Hearst, 1935–60; S. J. Phillips, Ltd., London, 1962; Peter Moores, Parbold Hall, Lancashire, 1962–72; S. J. Phillips, Ltd., London, 1972.
Literature: *Kratkoe Istoricheskoe Opisanie Kievo-Pecherskoi Lavry,* Kiev: Tipografia Akademii Kievskoi, 1805, p. 39 (in Russian); Evgeni, Metropolitan of Kiev and Galizia, *Opisanie Kievo-Pecherskoi Lavry,* Kiev: Kievo-Pecherskaia Lavra, 1826, p. 71 (in Russian); E. E. Bolkhovitinov, *Opisanie Kievo-Pecherskoi Lavry,* Kiev: Kievo-Pecherskaia Lavra, 1831, p. 86 (in Russian); "Cathedral Gates in Silver Gilt," *The Antique Collector,* April 1961, p. 66; M. Z. Petrenko, *Ukrainske Zolotarstvo XVI–XVIII,* Kiev: Naukova Dumka, 1969, pp. 139, 161 (in Ukrainian).

Exhibitions

Silver Plate of the Duke of Cumberland, Messrs. Crichton of Bond Street, London, 1924—cat. no. 23.

Corporate Plate of England and Wales, Goldsmiths' Hall, London, 1952—cat. no. 29 (pl. XXXVIII).

Silver by Paul de Lamerie in America, The Museum of Fine Arts, Houston, 10 November–2 December 1956—cat. nos. 12, 16 (repr.).

West County Treasures, City Art Gallery, Bristol, Summer 1967—cat. no. 17.

One Hundred Years of English Silver, University Art Museum, Austin, 21 September–22 October 1969—cat. no. 12 (one of pair repr.).

Silver Exhibition, Fitzwilliam Museum, Cambridge, 1969—cat. no. 2.

Mr. and Mrs. Morrie A. Moss Collection of Paul Storr Silver, 1771–1843, Brooks Memorial Art Gallery, Memphis, 3 December 1971–16 January 1972—cat. no. 29 (p. 20, 2 ills.).

Paul Storr Silver in American Collections, Indianapolis Museum of Art, February–March 1972—cat. nos. 21, 23.

Monumental Silver: The Gilbert Collection, Los Angeles County Museum of Art, 15 January–12 May 1974—cat. nos. 1–4, 9, 10, 15, 16, 18 (repr.), 19, 21, 24–26, 27 (repr.), 29, 30, 33–35, 38, 39, 42–44.

Monumental Silver and Mosaics: The Gilbert Collections, Los Angeles County Museum of Art, 14 January–28 December 1975—cat. nos. 1–5, 9, 10, 15, 16, 17 (repr.), 18 (repr.), 19, 21, 24–26, 27 (repr.), 29, 30, 33–36, 38, 39, 42–44.

A Decade of Collecting, Los Angeles County Museum of Art, 8 April–25 June 1975—cat. nos. 2 (p. 189, repr. p. 81), 17 (pp. 189–90, repr. p. 82), 43 (pp. 191–92, repr. pp. 84–85), 44 (p. 192–93, repr. p. 86).

Bibliography

Allen, Beverly Sprague, *Tides in English Taste (1619–1800): A Background for the Study of Literature,* Cambridge: Harvard University Press, vols. I and II.

Amelung, W., *Die Sculpturen des Vaticanischen Museum,* Berlin, 1908, vol. II.

Andrews, Alexander, *The Eighteenth Century or Illustrations of the Manners and Customs of Our Grandfathers,* London: Chapman and Hall, 1856.

Aresty, Esther B., *The Best Behavior,* New York: Simon and Schuster, 1970.

Banister, Judith (introduction), and Clark, Mark A. (catalog), *Paul Storr Silver in American Collections,* Indianapolis Museum of Art, 7 February–12 March 1972, and Dayton Art Institute, 24 March–30 April 1972.

Botsford, Jay Barrett, *English Society in the Eighteenth Century,* New York: Macmillan Co., 1924.

Burton, Elizabeth, *The Georgians at Home, 1714–1830,* London: Longmans, 1967.

Carritt, David, and Grimwade, Arthur, et al., *Christie's Review of the Year* (October 1964–July 1965), Christie's: London, 1965.

Clayton, Michael, *The Collector's Dictionary of the Silver and Gold of Great Britain and North America,* London: *Country Life,* The Hamlyn Publishing Group, 1971.

Dodds, John W., *The Age of Paradox: A Biography of England, 1841–1851,* New York: Rinehart and Co., Inc., 1952.

Edwards, Ralph, and Ramsey, L. G. G., eds., *The Early Georgian Period, 1714–1760,* vol. III, *The Late Georgian Period, 1760–1810,* vol. IV, *The Regency Period, 1810–1830,* vol. V, New York: Reynal and Co., 1958.

R. Garrard & Co., *Descriptive Inventory of Various Services of Plate,* London, 1872.

Graham, John Meredith, II (introduction), Buhler, Kathryn C. (silver catalog), and Austin, John C. (ceramics catalog), *The Campbell Museum Collection,* 2nd ed., rev. and enlarged, Camden: The Campbell Museum, 1972.

Grimwade, Arthur G., F. S. A., *Rococo Silver 1725–1765,* London: Faber and Faber, 1974.

Grimwade, Arthur G., F. S. A., *London Goldsmiths 1697–1837: Their Marks and Lives,* London: Faber and Faber, 1976.

Hayward, J. F., *Huguenot Silver in England, 1688–1727,* London: Faber and Faber, Ltd., 1959.

Hillier, Bevis, "The Gilbert Collection of Silver," *Connoisseur,* CXCII, no. 772, June 1976.

Honour, Hugh, *Goldsmiths and Silversmiths,* New York: G. P. Putnam's Sons, 1971.

Honour, Hugh, *The Age of Neo-classicism,* The Royal Academy and The Victoria and Albert Museum, London, 9 September–19 November 1972, London: The Arts Council of Great Britain, 1972.

Hope, Thomas, *Household Furniture and Interior Decoration* [1807], New York: Dover Pub. Inc., 1971.

Jackson, Sir Charles, *An Illustrated History of English Plate.* London, 1911, vols. I–II.

Jewitt, L., and St. John Hope, W. H., *Corporation Plate and Insignia of Office,* London, 1895, vol. I, pp. 327–28.

Jones, Edward Alfred, *Catalogue of Collection of Emperor of Russia,* London, 1909.

Jones, Edward Alfred, *The Gold and Silver of Windsor Castle,* Letchworth: Arden Press, 1911.

Jones, H. P., ed., *Dictionary of Foreign Phrases and Classical Quotations,* Edinburgh: John Grant, 1929.

Knocker, E. Wollaston, *An Account of the Corporation Insignia Seal and Plate,* Dover, 1898.

McKendry, Maxine, *The Seven Centuries Cookbook,* New York: McGraw-Hill Book Co., 1973.

Miles, Elizabeth B., *The Elizabeth B. Miles Collection: English Silver,* Hartford: Wadsworth Atheneum, 1976.

Moss, Morris A., *The Lillian and Morrie A. Moss Collection of Paul Storr Silver,* Miami: Roskin Book Production, 1972.

Musgrave, Clifford, *Life in Brighton,* London: Faber and Faber, 1970.

Myres, John L., *Catalogue of a Loan Exhibition of Silver Plate Belonging to the Colleges of the University of Oxford,* Oxford: Clarendon Press, 1928.

Oman, Charles C., *English Domestic Silver,* London: A&C Black, Ltd., 1934.

Oman, Charles C. (introduction), *Corporation Plate of England and Wales,* London: Goldsmiths' Hall, 1952.

Oman, Charles C., *English Silversmiths' Work Civil and Domestic: An Introduction,* Victoria and Albert Museum, London, 1965.

Osborne, Harold, ed., *The Oxford Companion to The Decorative Arts,* Oxford: Clarendon Press, Oxford University Press, 1975.

Penzer, N. M., *Paul Storr 1771–1844: Silversmith and Goldsmith,* London: B. T. Batsford, Ltd., 1954.

Penzer, N. M., "The Warwick Vase," *Apollo,* LXII, 1955, pp. 183–88 (pt. I); LXIII, 1955, pp. 18–22 (pt. II); and LXIII, 1956, pp. 71–75 (pt. III).

Phillips, Philip A. S., *Paul De Lamerie: Citizen and Goldsmith of London, A Study of His Life and Work A.D. 1688–1757,* London: B. T. Batsford, Ltd., 1935.

Pilcher, Donald, *The Regency Style, 1800–1830,* London: B. T. Batsford, Ltd., 1948.

Piranesi, Giovanni Battista, *Vasi, Candelabri, Cippi,* Rome, 1778.

Priestley, J. B., *The Prince of Pleasure and His Regency,* New York: Harper & Row, 1969.

Reade, Brian, *Regency Antiques,* London: B. T. Batsford, Ltd., 1953.

Reitlinger, Gerald, *The Economics of Taste,* New York: Holt, Rinehart and Winston, 1965.

Richardson, A. E., *Georgian England,* New York: Charles Scribner's Sons, 1931.

Russell, John, *Christie's Bi-Centenary Review of the Year* (October 1965–July 1966), Christie's: London, 1966.

Udy, David, "The Neo-Classicism of Charles Heathcote Tatham," *Connoisseur,* vol. CLXXVII, pp. 269–76.

Williams, E. N., *Life in Georgian England,* London: B. T. Batsford, Ltd., 1962.

Wilson, Philip, ed., *Art at Auction: The Year at Sotheby's and Parke-Bernet, 1966–67,* New York: American Heritage Publishing Co., Inc., 1967.

Wilson, Philip, ed., *Art at Auction: The Year at Sotheby's and Parke-Bernet, 1969–70,* New York: A Studio Book, The Viking Press, 1971.

Wilson, Philip, and Macdonald, Annamaria, eds., *Art at Auction: The Year at Sotheby's and Parke-Bernet, 1970–71,* New York: A Studio Book, The Viking Press, 1972.

Wintersgill, Donald, *English Antiques: The Age of Elegance, 1700–1830,* New York: William Morrow and Company, Ltd., 1975 (published in England as *The Guardian Book of Antiques, 1700–1830*).

Wyler, Seymour B., *The Book of Old Silver, English, American, Foreign,* New York: Crown, 1937.